Step by Step Art 4

for Upper Key Stage 2 Classes

by Dianne Williams

Published by

Topical Resources

Acknowledgement

The author and publisher would like to acknowledge the contribution made by the staff and pupils of the following schools during the preparation of this book. All teacher pages have been tested in the classroom. All photographed work has been produced by 9, 10 and 11 year old children working in a classroom situation.

Avondale Primary School, Darwen.
Beetham C.E. Primary School, Milnthorpe, Cumbria.
Coppice Primary School, Heanor, Derbyshire.
Feniscowles Primary School, Blackburn.
Griffin Park C.P. School, Blackburn.
Grove Park Primary School, Chiswick.
Hindsford C.E. Primary School, Atherton, Manchester.
Leeming and Londonderry C.P. School, Northallerton.
Middle Barton County Primary School, Chipping Norton, Oxfordshire.
Moor Park Junior School, Blackpool.
Otley Primary School, Ipswich.
Snape Community Primary School, North Yorkshire.
St. Gabriels C.E. School, Blackburn
St. Kentigern's R.C. Primary School, Blackpool.
Stanley Junior School, Blackpool.
Sudell County Primary School, Darwen.

Step by Step Art Books 1-4 are available from all good Educational Bookshops and by mail order from:

Topical Resources, P.O. Box 329,
Broughton,
Preston,
Lancashire.
PR3 5LT

Topical Resources publishes a range of Educational Materials for use in Primary Schools and Pre-School Nurseries and Playgroups.

For the latest catalogue   Tel 01772 863158
Fax 01772 866153
e.mail: sales@topical-resources.co.uk
Visit our Website at: www.topical-resources.co.uk

Printed in Great Britain for "Topical Resources", Publishers of Educational Materials, P.O. Box 329, Broughton, Preston, Lancashire PR3 5LT by T.Snape & Company Limited, Boltons Court, Preston Lancashire.

Typeset by Paul Sealey Illustration & Design, 3 Wentworth Drive, Thornton, Lancashire.

First Published September 2000.

ISBN 1 872977 54 5

Contents

Drawing

Painting

Printing

Collage

Sculpture

Textiles

Introduction

This book is intended for teachers of children in upper Key Stage Two classes to help them develop their 'pupils creativity and imagination through increasingly sustained activities, which build on their skills in using a range of materials and processes' (Art and Design Curriculum 2000).

It covers the new Programme of study for Key Stage Two using the same skill-based approach introduced in the previous books- Step By Step Art One (for the Under Fives), Step By Step Art Two (for Key Stage One) and Step By Step Art Three (for Lower Key Stage Two). As before the sessions are planned to introduce children to a wide range of tools and techniques, to encourage language and discussion, to use, build on and extend previous skills as well as developing further skills in a sequential series of activities. The areas of drawing, painting, printing, collage, sculpture and textiles are all targeted and the visual elements of art ie the language of the subject - line, tone, texture etc identified in relation to each session. Links are made with the work of other artists, craftworkers and designers 'from different times and cultures, eg: in Western Europe and the wider world' (Curriculum 2000).

As in the previous book (Step by Step Art Three) each session has a section on sketchbook work as pupils at Key Stage Two are still required 'to collect and record visual and other information in a sketchbook' (Curriculum 2000).

Each individual session and its extension activities could be used in isolation or form part of a progressive series of six lessons that focus on one media area at a time. The materials needed for each session are listed at the top of each page and the suppliers from whom they can be purchased are listed at the end of each section. All the sessions have been tried out in schools and demonstrate the achievements of children using the ideas in the book. To these children and their teachers I should like to express my appreciation and thanks.

Dianne Williams

Drawing

Drawing

Session One

Activity Scaling up and Scaling down - Using a Grid

Focus Shape and Space.

Equipment Needed
Drawing pencils (4b-6b), FreeArt paper (80gsm) A3 size, Larger than A3, Smaller than A4, Rulers, Black and white images (portraits or simple objects) cut from newspapers or magazines.1cm squared maths paper cut into pieces that are smaller than A4 (for sketch book work only).

Talk About
• What enlarging (scaling up) means.
• What reducing (scaling down) means.
• How to enlarge or reduce an image using the photocopier.
• Other things we have enlarged eg photographs.
• Other means of enlarging -Over head projectors, magnifying glasses etc.
• Finding enlarged and reduced images of the same picture eg Book covers often have a smaller version of the cover image on the flyleaf or the back cover.
• Postcards of paintings etc usually show the work on a much smaller scale than the original. Look on the back of some to discover the actual size of the work.

Sketchbook Work
Make a collection of simple black and white images from magazines or newspapers. Choose one, scale it up slightly and reduce it slightly using the photocopier. Stick the three images in your sketchbook, label the original and by how much the other two have been changed. Look up the words scale, enlarge, reduce, grid and record what they mean. Choose a piece of 1 cm squared maths paper and make a numbered grid.Along the top edge of your maths paper will be a series of squares. Start at the left hand side leave one square blank, then write a number in each of the other squares starting with 1 until you reach the end of the row. Numbers 10 upwards must not be split ie 10 goes in one square, 11 in the next etc.When you have reached the end of the row return to the start and begin to number the squares down the left hand side, top to bottom. Leave one on the top row as it was ie blank and start with the one below it, this will be another number 1 then 2 etc as before until you reach the bottom of the page. Try reading your grid - eg find square 3 line three (the numbers across the top identify the squares, the ones down the side identify the rows). You are now going to draw a grid like this on a black and white image to copy.

Doing
Choose a simple black and white image you would like to copy. Mount the picture on paper leaving a white border around the edge. Divide the picture into squares using your ruler and measuring carefully. Don't make the squares too small or your grid will be difficult to follow - and you will need to draw the same grid ie number of squares on your working piece of paper. Number the squares in the same way as you did in your sketch book (along the top of the black and white image and down the side of it - NOT ON IT). For your working piece of paper choose a piece that is similar in shape to the image you are going to copy ie a rectangle or a square but larger in size as you are going make an enlarged drawing. The working paper now needs a grid drawn on it, the squares need to be the same in number but larger in size than the ones you drew on your black and white image. The numbering across the top and down the side also needs to match that beside the black and white image. Use a drawing pencil and follow the squares on the image to copy and match what you see in the corresponding squares on your working paper. Copy one complete row at a time. You should end up with a copy of the original image but on a larger scale.If you worked using the same image and numbered grid but matched the drawing on a much smaller piece of paper you would end up with a copy on a smaller scale.

Developing the Idea
• Make a copy on an A1 piece of paper.
• Make a copy on a stamp sized piece of paper. Make 3 copies each of a different size from the same image eg: 3 bears
• Use this grid approach to copy the work of another artist - enlarge it or reduce it, or both. Alternatively use a drawing of your own.
• Record how to enlarge and reduce using a grid in your sketch book.

Links with the work of Other Artists
Drawings in comics and cartoons.
Photographs and their enlargements.
Claus Oldenburg

Drawing

Session   Two

Activity   Distortions and Reflections

Focus   Shape and Tone

Equipment Needed

Drawing pencils (4b-6b), White chalk or Chalk pastel, Charcoal or black pastel, Free Art paper (80gsm) A4 and A3 size, Rulers, Black and white Images (portraits or simple objects) cut from newspapers or magazines, 1 cm squared maths paper cut into pieces that are smaller than A4 (for sketchbook work only), Oil pastels and coloured chalk pastels, Grey sugar paper A4 and A3 size, Tin foil, Metal spoons, Tools with a reflective surface eg old irons, kettles etc. Non- reflective coloured objects eg: a ceramic mug to place on the foil and draw.

Talk About

• What distortion means and what reflection means.
• Where we see reflected images and what reflects them eg: mirrors, still water, shiny surfaces etc
• Where we see distorted images and what distorts them eg curved shiny surfaces, fairground mirrors, rippled water etc
• How to draw and number a grid on a black and white image as in the previous session and how to follow and copy the image from that grid.
• Changing the shape (distorting the grid) on your working paper.
• How this will alter (distort) the copied image eg: flatten it, make it tall and thin etc.

Sketchbook Work

Make a collection of pictures of reflections to stick in your sketchbook and write about them. Make a list of things you can see your reflection in and those that distort your reflection. Make a collection of shiny papers. Practice numbering a grid on a piece of squared maths paper as you did in the previous session. Draw three large squares to turn into different grids. One needs curved lines horizontally and vertically to create curved grid, one needs lines to create tall thin rectangles rather than squares, one needs lines to create flat broad rectangles rather than squares. These grids need numbering in the same way as the squared grid. You might want to try drawing other grids of your own on a scrap of paper, to stick in your sketch book later. Try all the different drawing media on offer - write their names, what they feel like to draw with and the sort of marks, blends, smudges, lights and darks they will make.

Doing

As in the previous session choose a simple black and white image, mount it and divide it into a squared numbered grid (Don't make the squares too small or make too many of them). Choose a pencil and a piece of Free Art paper similar in shape to your image, ie a rectangle or square. On this you are going to draw a different grid eg a curved or stretched grid. It MUST have the same number of shapes to draw in as the grid on your b/w image and be numbered in the same way for you to copy the image. Follow the squares and match what you see in the corresponding shapes on your working paper. Copy and complete one row at a time. You should end up with a distorted copy of your original image.

For another distorted image, look at your face reflected in the back of a spoon. Choose a piece of grey sugar paper and b/w pastels to draw with. First draw a large outline of the shape of the spoon, now look at what is reflected in the centre of it (and how it is distorted) and add that to your drawing, then look at either edge of your reflection and add that. Remember to look and record carefully changes of shape and size to create a distorted reflection.

For another distorted reflection place a coloured object on a piece of foil in such that reflects both the back and the sides of the object. If you crease the foil slightly the reflection becomes more distorted. Choose either oil pastels or chalk pastels to draw with on grey sugar paper.

Developing the Idea

• Explore copying images on other styles of distorted grids.
• Draw tools eg an egg whisk, with shiny and reflective surfaces.
• Draw distorted reflections in other shiny objects eg: a bottle or a kettle.
• Draw the merging distorted reflections of several objects on a piece of foil.

Links with the work of Other Artists

Escher
Victor Vasarly
David Hockney

Drawing

Session Three

Activity Composition - Arranging Shapes Lines and Colours

Focus Shape and Space

Equipment Needed

A4 pieces of black paper and white paper, scissors, glue, postcards of still life and abstract paintings by other artists, Drawing pencils (4b - 6b), oil pastels, wax crayons, chalk pastels -to offer choice, view finders, assorted packaging and advertisements, magazines, FreeArt paper (80gsm) cut to match the shape of the viewfinders ie square or rectangular(A4 or 21x21 cm), objects man-made or natural to arrange in a 'composition'.

Talk About

- What 'composition' means ie harmonious relationships within an art work, the skilful arrangement of lines shapes and spaces.
- The composition within the work of another artist eg which part do you look at first, are the shapes symmetrical or intentionally unbalanced, are they large or small, plain or decorated, grouped, isolated or joined by lines, do the lines convey a mood or feeling etc?
- Points to look for: note these in a sketchbook
- A dark shape or a large shape will appear heavier than a light shape or a small shape.
- A small dark shape can balance a large light one.
- A patterned or textured shape will appear heavier than a smooth shape.
- A small textured shape can balance a large smooth one.
- Several small shapes can balance a large shape.
- Space can help balance an object - it is also better to use an odd number of objects in a composition.
- Unbalanced compositions are often used to create a feeling of unease, humour or movement.

Sketchbook Work

Look up the word composition and write down what it means.Record the 'points to look for' discussed in the Talk About session. Use the black paper and scissors to cut out shapes of different sizes and 'compose' them in the ways suggested above. Stick your compositions in sketchbook and describe their arrangement. For patterned or textured shapes make rubbings on the white paper before you cut the shapes out. Cut several objects out of magazines and arrange them in a new composition. Describe the composition of lines shapes and spaces in a picture you like by another artist - remember to record the artists name and the title of the picture.

Doing

Take a viewfinder, a coloured advertisement or piece of packaging, a pencil and a piece of FreeArt paper that matches the shape of your viewfinder but is larger in size. Use your viewfinder to select an area with an interesting balance of colours and shapes. Look at several views before you make your final decision. Copy the outline of the shapes you see on your larger piece of paper. You are now ready to add colour. You are going to choose which drawing media to use to match the colours you see. You may need to try several or even to blend colours to get an ideal match. Record the colours you need, what you used and how you made them in your sketchbook.

Choose an abstract or still life painting by another artist. Copy some of the shapes you see in their composition, match their size carefully and colour them to match the original. Cut these shapes out and on a new piece of paper arrange them in a different way. Try several different compositions before you stick them down. Add your own background / foreground / setting.

Developing the Idea

- Cut the shapes out that match a picture as before but this time when you re-arrange them don't use all the shapes. Leave some out and add some new ones of your own to complete the composition.
- Explore making different arrangements with the same shapes each time, using a computer. Save some of your compositions and print them out.
- Choose some real objects to arrange as a still life composition. When you are happy with your arrangement make a rough sketch of your composition.
- Give the same objects to a friend to arrange in a different way. Record the new arrangement.
- Make a class or group composition with several children adding an object and arranging it to fit in to the whole. Discuss each new addition and the appropriateness of its position-things may need to be moved around before everyone is satisfied! Sketch the final composition.

Links with the work of Other Artists

Paul Cezanne
Henri Matisse
Braque

Drawing

Session Four

Activity Portraits and Proportion

Focus Line, Shape, Tone, Colour and Texture

Equipment Needed
Drawing Pencils (4b-6b),Black and White Chalk pastels, Coloured Chalk pastels, Wax Crayons, Coloured pencils, Mirrors if the portraits are to be self -portraits, FreeArt Paper (80gsm) or Grey sugar paper cut to A3 size. Larger paper for full length portraits.

Talk About
• The difference between a portrait and a self-portrait
• Paper held portrait way up or landscape way up.
• Looking carefully at the proportions of a head and where the features fit eg a head is roughly an oval shape and is symmetrical. The eyes are in the centre and the nose is halfway between the eyes and the chin. The mouth is half-way between the nose and the chin. The top of the ears are level with the eyes and the bottom level with the base of the nose. The eyes are roughly one eyes width apart and the iris is not round as it is partially covered by the upper and lower eye lids.
• Note these pointers in your sketchbook. Look at portraits by other artists to see if they have used these pointers.

Sketchbook Work
Draw several ovals in your sketchbook. Cut eyes for one oval (from a newspaper) a nose for another, a mouth for another etc. Place them in the correct position on each oval and draw in the additional features to complete each portrait. Make a list of portraits painted by other artists and the names of the sitters. Describe your favourite and why you like it. Make a black and white photocopy of a head and shoulders picture of yourself. Draw a frame to go round it. Make a list of body proportions to be aware of should you draw a full length figure - NB: The top of the legs is halfway up the body. The head is about one sixth of the body and the shoulders are twice the width of the head. The arms are as long as the legs, the feet are as long as the head and the hands are as long as the face. The hands reach to mid thigh. The elbow is at the centre of the arm and the knee is at the centre of the leg. Arms are joined to the shoulders and don't sprout from the neck. When a figure is seated the distance from shoulder to seat is the same as from the back of the seat to the knee. Look for standing and sitting full length portraits by other artists and make a list of them.

Charlotte

Doing
Choose a drawing pencil and a piece of A3 white paper or b/w chalk pastels and a piece of grey sugar paper. Turn the paper so that it is portrait way up. Look at your subject carefully. Trace the shape of their face with your finger only on your piece of paper to see where it will fit - remember to leave room for the hair, the neck and the shoulders. Lightly sketch in the shape of the head, the neck and the shoulders. Now lightly sketch in the eyes, nose, mouth etc carefully matching the shapes you can see and placing them in the right position (NB each person is different). Now you are ready to add detail and interest by looking for shadows, lines, creases, curves and textures and of course colours. You may want to experiment with shading (pressing on), smudging and different sort of lines (fine, thick, curling, twisting, spiky etc) on a scrap of paper or in your sketchbook to get the right effect before you add them to your portrait. List the colours you need to match before you start finding and making them. You may need to use more than one drawing media to get the effect you want. When the head is complete add detail to the chin, under the chin and to the clothes around the neck and covering the shoulders.

Developing the Idea
• Try working with a mirror in front of you and draw a self portrait.
• Draw a portrait from observation but use the style of another artist eg Van Gogh, Lowry or Picasso.
• Draw a portrait of a friend dressed in unusual clothes, wearing a hat or in a costume similar to that worn in a portrait by another artist.
• Draw a portrait in profile.
• Draw a full length portrait of a friend standing facing you.
• Draw a full length portrait of a friend sitting on a chair either facing you or in profile.
• Sit a doll or a puppet to lean against a box and draw it.

Links with the work of Other Artists
Rembrandt
Picasso
Holbein
Frances Bacon

Drawing

Session Five

Activity Movement

Focus Line, Shape and Tone

Equipment Needed
Drawing pencils (4b-6b),FreeArt paper (80 gsm) cut to both A4 and A3 size, a range of coloured drawing media eg chalk pastels, wax crayons, oil pastels and pencil crayons to offer choice for extension work. Grey sugar paper cut to A3 size. Magazine and newspaper pictures that show moving figures - sports pages are a good starting point.

Talk About
- The ways in which the figures are moving in the pictures-running, jumping, batting, bowling etc. Make a collection of 'moving' words. Write them in your sketchbook.
- How the body shape appears, which bits are bent, which bits remain upright when a class member poses as one of these movements.
- Move round the pose and talk about how it appears when viewed from the side and the back. Discuss where limbs are jointed and can bend (elbows, ankles, wrists, knees).
- Describe the different movement's viewpoints-back views, side views, front views. Describe what you might see and record if you were drawing a picture of a P.E. lesson, at the swimming pool or children in the playground.

Sketchbook Work
Choose a magazine or newspaper picture of a group of people moving in different ways eg in the park, on the beach. Make a list next to the picture of all the different movements you can see. You could join these to each figure with an arrow. Choose one of these figures to draw as a stick man - draw a line for the spine, (this may need to bend forwards or backwards according to the pose you are copying) then sketch in oval shapes for the head, chest and hips to create a body. Add the arms to an oval at the top where the shoulders would be -do you need to make one or both bend up or down? Remember they can only bend at the elbows, it might be a good idea to draw a small circle on each arm to remind you where each arm can bend. The legs are next, these come from the sides of the hips and can only bend at the knees. It might be a good idea to add small circles to these to remind you where each leg can bend, they should be as big as the face and may need to point in different directions. Draw other 'moving' stick figures.

Doing
Choose a piece of A3 FreeArt Paper and a drawing pencil. One child needs to pose for the class as though he/she was moving eg running, for the others to make an outline sketch of their body, limbs, face and clothes. Choose another child to pose as though they were moving in a different way eg hopping. Make another outline sketch on the same piece of paper wherever you want - next to, behind, in front,-but this time from a different viewpoint (profile or back view). Choose a third child to pose in another way eg bending over and draw them again - either from the same or from a new viewpoint- wherever you want on the same piece of paper. You are now ready to add details to your drawings eg patterns or folds on clothes, shadows under chins, hair texture, shoe laces, ribbons, badges etc.

Developing the Idea
- Choose one of the moving figures to work on as a full length individual portrait on a piece of A3 paper portrait way up. Copy the same pose but add in a background that puts the pose in an appropriate setting.
- Develop any of the previous figures as a colour study allowing a choice of drawing media.
- Sketch in very lightly a background of your choice. Give it to a friend to add an appropriate group of moving figures to it.
- Collect sketches of moving figures (in your sketchbook) by observation at playtime. Add those you are most pleased with to a large scale collaborative drawing of a picture entitled 'Playtime'.

Links with the work of Other Artists
Seurat - The Grande Jatte
Beryl Cook
Degas
L.S.Lowry

Drawing

Session   Six

Activity   Visual Jokes and Cartoons

Focus   Line and Shape

Equipment Needed

Drawing pencils (4b-6b), FreeArt paper (80 gsm), a range of coloured drawing media to offer choice, comics and newspaper cartoons of well known people.

Talk About

• The type of stimulus - familiar sayings - to be used as the starting point to tell a visual joke. Possible sayings that could be used eg Raining cats and dogs, Time flies, etc. Make a class collection of these before recording them in individual sketchbooks.

• The need to make these drawings amusing.

• Discuss what a cartoon is, favourite cartoon characters and the way these characters have exaggerated features. Look at cartoons of well known people and the sort of features the cartoonist exaggerates eg ears, teeth, chin.

• Look at pictures of well known people eg the Prime Minister and compare their real likeness and how they appear as an exaggerated and amusing cartoon image. Discuss what has been exaggerated?

Sketchbook Work

Choose one saying from your list that you might like to turn into a visual joke. Write down some of the things you might draw. Make rough sketches of them and how they might be arranged in a final drawing. Make sure the story is easy to understand and not confusing. The sketch will need to to be a simple one to give a clear message. You might want to sketch out several sayings before you are pleased with the result and are ready to develop it into a final piece of finished work. Make a collection of cartoon figures from comics and newspapers. Describe your favourite and why you like it. Cut some faces out of a newspaper or magazine and exaggerate their personality eg an extended hairstyle, bulging eyes, protruding ears etc. Make a collection of different eyes mouths that you think show different expressions eg surprise, anger etc Next to each one write down the emotion you think they show. Collect pictures of cartoon characters that also show different emotions - exaggerated style! Record which emotions these are. All this information will help you with you own cartoon drawing. You may have a computer programme that will also show examples of cartoons.

Doing

First you are going to work on your visual joke using the rough sketches you have made in your sketchbook.

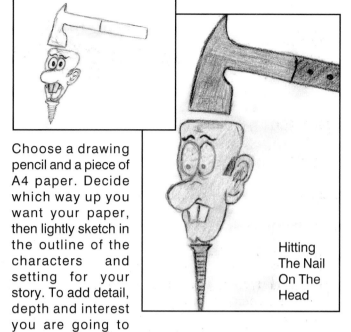

Choose a drawing pencil and a piece of A4 paper. Decide which way up you want your paper, then lightly sketch in the outline of the characters and setting for your story. To add detail, depth and interest you are going to

Hitting The Nail On The Head

develop it in colour. You are going to choose the coloured drawing media you want to use - it can be a combination of different sorts if you prefer. Show your finished picture to the class and see if they can understand and guess your visual joke. Other people may have worked on the same saying as you. If so you can compare similarities and differences.

For your cartoon drawing you are going to use a friend as a model. Look at them carefully before you start to sketch. Cartoonists often make the head much larger than it should be - this might be useful to remember if you are going to draw a full length figure. You could choose to draw only a head and shoulders cartoon. Take a drawing pencil and a piece of A4 paper and sketch in the outline of your friends head - leave space below it if you are going to add a body as well. Ask you friend to make their face appear eg happy, cross, puzzled etc and to hold that expression. You are now going to record that expression but exaggerate it. Their hairstyle can be exaggerated to match the mood too eg standing on end, becoming extra curly etc. If you are going to add a body this will need to show the same emotion in the way it poses -again exaggerated eg shoulders hunched up or drooping, arms and hands waving, clenched etc. Display the cartoon gallery and see if as a class the correct identity can be added to each drawing.

Developing the Idea

• Choose a picture of a sports personality or a pop star and draw a cartoon version of it.

• Print out a cartoon character from a computer programme and draw in a 'friend' to go with them. Use these two characters in a cartoon strip story of your own.

• Turn an animal into a cartoon character and invent a name for it. Make a short strip cartoon story using your character.

Links with the work of Other Artists

Cartoons and Comic Strips
Keith Haring
Quentin Blake
Comic Greetings Cards
Roy Lichenstein

Materials

Newsprint or FreeArt Paper 80gsm
Sketchbooks
Wax crayons
Drawing pencils 4b-6b
Squared Maths Paper
Oil pastels
Chalk Pastels
Grey Sugar Paper
Tin Foil
Black sugar Paper
Coloured Pencils

Suppliers

NES Arnold Ltd
Ludlow Hill Road
West Bridgeford
NOTTINGHAM
NG2 6HD

Pisces
Westwood Studies
West Avenue
CREWE
Cheshire
CW1 3AD

Philip & Tracey Ltd
North Way
Andover
Hampshire
SP10 5BA

Hope Education
Orb Mill
Huddersfield Road
OLDHAM
Lancashire
OL4 2ST

Yorkshire Purchasing Organisation
41 Industrial Park
WAKEFIELD
WF2 0XE

Drawing

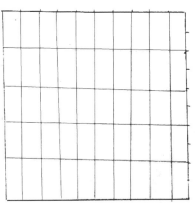

Sessions 1&2
Examples of
scaling up
and distorting

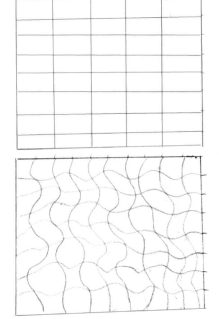

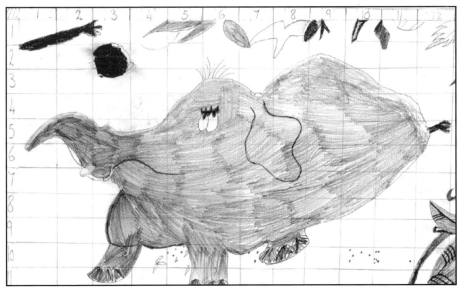

Drawing

Session 3
Example of a created composition.

Session 6   Example of a visual joke.

Session 4
Example portraits.

14

Painting

The Trouble With Trevor.
By Lee Wigley.

Session 1
Example of a painting with atmosphere.

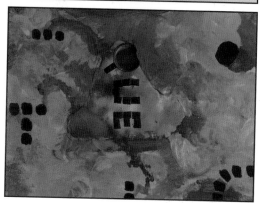

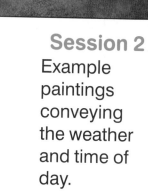

Session 2
Example paintings conveying the weather and time of day.

Painting

Session 4
Example of working
in the style of another
artist. (Picasso).

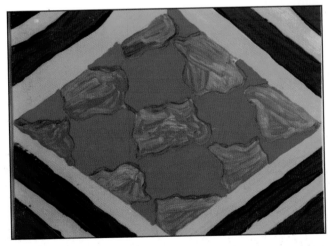

Session 5
Example of exploring colour groups
and contrasts.

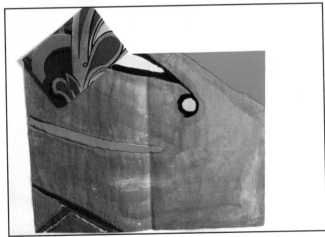

Session 6
Example of drawing with a brush.

Painting

Painting

There's Something Different About Jacqueline
By Emma Frost

Session One

Activity Creating Mood and Atmosphere

Focus Colour and Shape

Equipment Needed

Ready mix or powder paint - in either a single or dual primary system plus black and white, mixing palettes or pieces of card to use as mixing palettes, water pots, paper towels. FreeArt paper (80gsm) cut to A3 size, scrap paper on which to collect and name any colours mixed and how they were made - this will be stuck into sketchbooks later. Thick and thin brushes. Coloured wax crayons for sketchbook work.

Talk About

- Colours you would expect to find in a picture of a Haunted House, why these colours would be chosen and the feeling they would convey.
- Colours you would find in a picture of a Circus and the mood and atmosphere they would convey.
- What colours can do - you may agree or disagree, try and find examples in the work of other artists!
- Blue is cold and serene, it recedes into the distance and can convey calm, mystery or sadness. Yellow is hot and bright but add a touch of black and it can become sinister. Red is lively and energetic but also associated with anger and danger. Green is quiet and cool - a growing colour. Orange is warm giving a feeling of richness, where as purple is strong - add black and it conveys fear.

Sketchbook Work

List the colours discussed above and describe what they convey to you. Write the titles of work by other artists that convey a feeling to you, what that feeling is and how the artist has done it. Collect pictures from magazines that give you a frightened feeling, an excited feeling, a puzzled feeling, etc. Look at the colours in the pictures as well as the subject. Give each picture a title. To try out the effect of different colours make two outline sketches of the same house, use wax crayon to add colour and make one house a welcoming pleasant place to live, and the other a sinister, mysterious place to live. Make a list of your 'welcoming, pleasant' colours and another list of your 'sinister, mysterious' colours. Try the same approach using wax crayon to add to and change a black and white landscape picture from a magazine. Describe the colours you have used and the mood and atmosphere the altered image is intended to convey.

Doing

Imagine you are going to paint a picture for the cover of a book. The picture you paint and the colours you use will give a message about the type of story in the book. The book can be eg a Thriller, a Space adventure, a Murder Mystery, a Book of Fairy tales, a Book of Giants and Monsters, a book of Disasters, a Book of Magic and Enchantment etc. Choose which type of book you are going to design for but don't worry about giving it a title yet - you could print out the title on the computer later and use a style of type that matches the mood of the book. Use a card palette and a scrap piece of paper and try mixing and making the colours you feel will create the right mood for your type of book. Make a list of some of the things you want to draw on the cover. Choose a piece of A3 paper and a thin brush. You are going to draw an outline of the characters and setting for your book cover using a brush and a pale shade of grey paint - if you are unhappy with anything you will be able to paint over it later. Once your outline is done you can begin adding the other colours you plan to use to complete your book cover and convey the mood and atmosphere of the book.

Developing the Idea

- Give a friend the title for a picture they must paint that conveys a mood or atmosphere you have chosen.
- Paint a picture of a strange garden or a magic garden.
- Paint a picture of a landscape on an unfriendly planet and then a friendly planet.
- Paint a picture of a dense jungle, a weird wood or deep under the sea.
- Each member of the class paint from the same title eg Fire! Happiness, Fear or Peace. Compare the choice of colour and subject matter.

Links with the work of Other Artists

Book Illustrators
Magritte
Salvador Dali

Painting

Session   Two

Activity   Conveying the Weather and Time of Day

Focus   Colour, Shape, Line and Tone

Equipment Needed

Ready mix or powder paint - in either a dual or single primary system plus black and white, mixing palettes or pieces of card to use as mixing palettes, water pots, paper towels, FreeArt paper (80 gsm) cut to A3 size, scrap paper on which to collect and name any colours mixed - this will be stuck into sketchbooks later. Drawing pencils and thick and thin brushes. Wax crayons for sketchbook work. Oil pastels for overdrawing and adding detail to painting.

Talk About

- Different types of weather and colours associated with different types of weather.
- The colour of the sky, shadows, reflections, the colour of buildings, the clothes worn by figures and how they appear to move if it is eg sunny and warm, windy and stormy, rainy, cold and icy, foggy etc.
- Look at pictures by other artists and discuss the different types of weather in each and how the artist gives you that message.
- Which you feel is the most successful and why.
- Sorting a group of postcards into sets of different weather types.
- Monet's series of paintings of Rouen Cathedral.
- The different times of day the pictures show and how can you tell.
- What time of day are colours seen at their brightest.
- How colours change as it gets towards night time.

Sketchbook Work

Look out of the class room window and list some of the things you can see.
Draw some boxes and label them for different types of weather. On a sunny day record how the things on your list look (colourful, bright etc) and use wax crayon to record the colours you see. Do the same thing on a dull rainy day - and so on. Alternatively, make a record of the view early in the morning and late in the afternoon. In each case compare the different colours that you see in the same view. Collect magazine pictures that show different types of weather - stick some in your sketchbook, describe each type of weather you can see and the colours in the pictures. Look at the work of other artists and see if you can find four that show different types of weather. Record the name of each artist and the title of each picture. Discuss which is your favourite and why?

Doing

Decide which type of weather your picture is going to show and list the colours you might want to use. Choose a piece of scrap paper and when you have successfully mixed your colours record them and how you made them -this will go in your sketchbook later. You now need to decide on the subject for you picture if you choose a landscape- it could be your garden, the school building, a view through a window or doorway at school. Alternatively, you could choose people it could be - coming to school in the rain, or a snowy playtime, or jumping in puddles, a windy day in the park etc. When you have chosen your subject and found the colours you need you may want to sketch out some rough ideas for your painting in your sketchbook.
When you are ready to start your finished work, choose a piece of A3 paper, decide which way up you want it to be (landscape or portrait) and begin painting the main shapes in using a thin brush and pale grey paint - this will allow you to over paint and change your mind easily. Remember the shapes in the distance will be the smallest and those nearest to you will be the largest - those in the middle ground will be in -between. To fill in the shapes and add depth and interest you will need to use your 'weather colours', overdrawing to add detail can be done on top of the filled shapes using either a fine brush or oil pastels or both. Display the paintings without titles and ask the class to name them and the weather or time of day in each picture.

Developing the Idea

- Make a painting of the same scene but change the weather.
- All the class paint a scene set in the same weather conditions.
- Paint your favourite weather and what you like to do - and your least favourite weather.
- Paint a picture to go in a summer holiday brochure - and a winter holiday brochure.
- Paint a picture of Doctor Foster in a shower of rain for a Nursery Rhyme Book.

Links with the work of Other Artists

Monet
Renoir
J.M.W.Turner
James Whistler

Painting

Session   Three

Activity   Camouflage

Focus   Colour, Shape and Pattern

Equipment Needed

Ready mix or powder paint - in either a dual or single primary system plus black and white, mixing palettes or pieces of card to use as mixing palettes, water pots, paper towels, FreeArt paper cut to A4 and A3 size, scrap paper for initial colour work and for later collecting colours mixed and matched to complete a camouflage - this will be stuck into sketch books later. Scissors, coloured magazines and glue. Wax crayons for sketchbook work. Thick and thin brushes.

Talk About

• What the word 'camouflage' means.
• Animals, insects, birds and fish whose body colour and pattern helps them to merge into the background - and how this helps them.
• People who camouflage themselves - and why.
• How people camouflage themselves.
• How you might camouflage yourself in eg the snow, or a desert.
• Camouflaging objects by placing them on different surfaces and against different backgrounds.

Sketchbook Work

Look up the meaning of the word camouflage and write it down. Look in magazines for pictures of birds, insects, animals or fish that merge with their background and are camouflaged. Draw a camouflage outfit you might wear if you didn't want to be seen at night. Now draw an outfit you might wear if you wanted to be seen. Cut out a black and white picture of a car from a magazine. Use wax crayons to add colour and decoration to it to camouflage it for a trip to the jungle. Do the same to another picture of a car, this time imagine it needs to be camouflaged to go under the sea. Create a camouflage of your own for another car picture and describe where this one would be going.

Doing

Choose a small piece of scrap paper, a paint brush and some paints. You are not going to mix colours for your first camouflage just use them as they are. Make several shapes (about 6) of different colours - you can use the same colour more than once - on different parts of your paper. Some of the shapes can be joined together, others can be on their own. When the shapes are dry you need to cut them out and re-arrange them in groups on different parts of a new sheet of (A4) paper. When you are pleased with your arrangement you need to glue the shapes down. Give your paper to a friend in exchange for theirs. Look carefully at these new shapes - you are going to extend them and join them up so that the original shapes are camouflaged in an interesting way. You will be able to find the colours easily as they haven't been mixed. Take care to make your joined up camouflage an interesting shape - don't paint OVER any of the original shapes - you don't need to fill in all the paper. Once the shapes are joined and camouflaged -STOP! For your second camouflage you are going to mix and match colours. Cut out a small piece of a magazine picture - it doesn't need to show complete objects or people- just a section that has strong colours and shapes. Stick it in the middle of a new piece of A4 paper. You are now going to extend these shapes to the edge of the page. You will need to mix your colours carefully to make them match the cut out piece or the camouflage will fail. When you extend the shapes they can change eg get long and thin, curl and curve etc to make the new camouflaged shape more interesting. Fill the gaps around the camouflaged shape with any colours you choose.

Developing the Idea

• Use a piece of the reproduction of an artists work to camouflage and extend -colour photocopies A3 size from a postcard are easy to share between a class. They are only required to match and extend the colours and shapes they see, they do not need to make a picture.
• Use a cut out piece from a magazine picture, colour match the piece but turn it into something eg a flower or an insect.
• Stick an autumn leaf on a piece of paper and paint in the background using the same colours as the leaf and hopefully camouflage it.
• Cut out a picture of an animal or bird, stick it on a new piece of paper and add a background that camouflages it.

Links with the work of Other Artists

Wildlife Photographs
Picasso
Paul Klee

Painting

Session   Four

Activity   Working in the Style of Another Artist

Focus   Line, Shape, Colour, Pattern,
Scale and Texture

Equipment Needed
Drawing pencils (4b-6b), Ready mix or powder paint in either a dual or single primary system plus black and white, mixing palettes or pieces of card to use as mixing palettes, water pots, paper towels, viewfinders, FreeArt paper(80gsm) cut to A4 and A3 size, wax crayons for sketchbook work, scrap paper for initial colour work - this will be stuck into sketch books later. A selection of artists work in postcard form, from which to obtain the information as to the style of the artist. Thick and thin brushes.

Talk About
• The different styles seen in a range of work by different artists.
• A suggested group of artists to look at, discuss and use might include:-
  Van Gogh - for line, colour and texture.
  Seurat - for colour, shape and texture applied through dots.
  Lowry - for colour and shape and mood.
  Georgia O'Keefe - for scale and viewpoint.
  Picasso - for colour and shape.
  Klimt - for colour and pattern.
• What information they might collect to use in a piece of work of their own.
• The subject of each artist's work - landscape, portrait, built environment, still life etc.
• Using a viewfinder to isolate different parts of an artists work to collect information and recording the information in a sketchbook.
• Using the same subject as the artist but not copying the original eg a new portrait using the same shapes and colours identified and selected from portraits by Picasso.
• Using a different subject but painting it in the style of an artist eg Sports Day in the style of Seurat, building the painting up using only dots and placing them closely together.

Sketchbook Work
Choose a picture by an artist whose style you want to copy. Record the name of the artist and the title of the work plus any other details about the artist that you can discover eg date of birth, place of birth, friends, style of work, famous or well known paintings, date of death etc.

Use a viewfinder on the picture you want to use and decide what you are going to collect. Make a list eg colours, shapes, lines, patterns etc. Draw a box for each of the items on your list. Draw what you have found for each one.

Doing
Decide what the subject of your 'In the Style of' picture is going to be - a new version of a similar subject, a different subject but using the colours, lines and shapes in the same way as another artist or copying a picture from a magazine as though a particular artist had painted it. You must NOT COPY an original artists work but your must show in your own work that you have looked carefully at what they have done and you can use the same approach as them - but in your own way. You might want to try a few ideas out in rough sketches in your sketch book. When you feel ready to start - on either a piece of A3 or A4 paper- use a thin paint brush and a pale shade of paint to mark out the main shapes. As you build up your painting you will need to look at your sketchbook to make sure the style (lines, colours, textures etc) that you add match those of the artist you looked at. Display all the finished paintings and make a collection of the artist's pictures on postcard that have been used. Have a session when different members of the class try to find the postcard of an artists work/style that matches each painting- and give their reason why.

Developing the Idea
• All the class work in the style of the same artist.
• All the class paint a portrait or self portrait in the style of the same artist - or in the style of several different artists.
• Set up a still life using the same objects observed in an artists work eg Cezanne, and paint it from observation.
• Paint the same still life but use the colours, lines and textures of another artist.
• Paint a holiday postcard that an artist might send - in their own particular style.

Links with the work of Other Artists
Picasso
Modigliani
Van Gogh

Painting

Session   Five

Activity   Exploring Colour Groups and Contrasts.

Focus   Colour

Equipment Needed
Ready mix or powder paint in either a dual or single primary system plus black and white, mixing palettes or pieces of card to use as mixing palettes, water pots, paper towels, FreeArt paper(80 gsm) cut to A4 and A3 size, wax crayons for sketchbook work. Scrap paper for initial colour mixing. Brushes.

Talk About
Colour groups and the colour wheel.

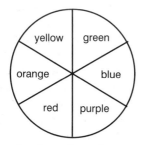

- The position of colours found on a colour wheel.
- Primary Colours - red, blue and yellow. These form the basis of all other colours. They cannot be made by mixing.
- Secondary colours - (orange, green, purple). These are mixtures of any two primary colours.
- Complimentary colours. These are found opposite each other on the colour wheel. They stand out from each other and do not blend together. (eg red and green, purple and yellow, orange and blue)
- Harmonious colours are those that are next to each other on the colour wheel. They are pleasing to the eye when they are together.

Sketchbook Work
Look up the meaning of 'harmony', 'complementary' and 'contrast' and write it in your sketchbook. Make a coloured strip of primary colours using wax crayons. Write down their names. Make a coloured strip of secondary colours using wax crayons. Write down their names. Draw a circle and divide it into six parts. Colour it in to show the colours that contrast each other, opposite each other. Write down their names. Draw a circle and put the tertiary colours round the edge - these will be primary, secondary and primary + secondary. You might need to list the colours and the order they go in first. If there is a book about colour or painting in the library it may show a picture of the colour wheel or circle that would help you.

Doing
Pictures that use harmonious colours (colours close to each other on the colour wheel) are very pleasing because the colours support each other.

Pictures that use complementary colours are strong and vibrant. Look for magazine pictures and postcards of artists work that are in harmonious colours or complementary colours. You are going to paint a picture of the same thing twice, once in two contrasting colours and once in two harmonious colours. Choose the colours from the two groups that you are going to use and practice mixing them on a palette - you will need to keep the two groups quite separate. Take a piece of A4 paper and draw in pale paint the outline of the shapes in your picture. Keep it simple as you will need to draw the same outline again on another piece of A4 paper. A face, a flower, a fish or a house are possible ideas. Fill in the shapes on one paper using the two harmonious colours and on the other in the two contrasting colours. Compare and discuss the effect. Display the work in two blocks - one of pictures using harmonious colours the other of pictures using contrasting colours. There should be quite a difference.

Developing the Idea
- All the children paint a portrait using two contrasting colours.
- Paint a pattern half in two harmonious colours and half in contrasting colours.
- Make an observational drawing of a view around school and photocopy it. Fill one of the drawings with harmonious colours and the other with two contrasting colours.
- Make a patchwork of individual patterned squares, some squares will need to be patterned in harmonious colours only, others in contrasting colours only.

Links with the work of Other Artists
Andy Warhol
Dufy
Derain
Robert Delauney

Painting

Session   Six

Activity   Drawing with a Brush

Focus   Shape, Colour, Pattern and Texture

Equipment Needed

Ready mix or powder paint in either a single or dual primary system plus black and white, mixing palettes or pieces of card to use as mixing palettes, water pots, paper towels, thick and thin brushes, FreeArt paper (80 gsm) cut to A3 size, wax crayons for sketchbook work. Scrap paper for initial colour mixing. A bunch of flowers, flowers in a vase or a group of different fruits to arrange as a still life stimulus. Drawing pencils (4b-6b).

Talk About

- The composition of shapes in the still life arrangement. How they appear in position and scale and whether some shapes are slightly hidden by others.
- The colours in the still life arrangement, pale or bright - or both? dark or light? Are they all different or are there several shades of some colours?
- Describe any textures you can see.
- Describe any patterns you can see.
- Look at the direction the shapes bend or curve.
- Can you see both the back and the front of any of the shapes.
- Do the shapes cast a shadow?
- What is underneath the shapes?

Sketchbook Work

Make rough outline sketches of some of the individual shapes you can see in the still life in front of you. Then make an outline sketch of the group of shapes you can see and how they are arranged next to each other, in front of each other and behind each other. Some will be bigger than others, some smaller, and some shapes you may only be able to see little or part of. Look carefully - and keep on looking!- whilst you sketch. Make several drawings of the same still life from different viewpoints. You will then need to choose one of your sketches to be copied and developed as a finished piece of work.

Make a list of the colours you can see in the still life objects and try and make and match them using wax crayon. Record which colours you blended together if you needed to make a new colour. Look up the word 'still life' and write down what it means. Find four still life paintings by other artists. Write down their titles and the name of each artist.

Doing

Choose a palette, a medium/thick brush and a piece of A3 paper. Look at the sketch you are going to copy. Touch the shapes you have drawn with your finger then draw them again but larger (again with your finger) on your A3 paper. This will give you a feel for the space on the paper that you have to use and the size that you will be able to make the group of shapes. Mix the main colour you see on one of the shapes - the largest or smallest would be a good starting point as you will be able to relate the other shapes to it. Draw that shape with your brush and fill it in with the one colour you have made. Now choose another shape, mix the main colour for it, and draw and fill it in its position in the group. Continue until all the shapes have been copied from your sketch, drawn and filled with their one main colour. Now you are ready to return to each shape in turn and mix and add more of the colours you can see on each one. You may want to change your brush to draw in some details. Add pattern or texture- a fine brush will let you draw these in more easily. Keep dabs of the colours you have made and how you made them on a scrap piece of paper to go in your sketchbook

Developing the Idea

- Set up a still life in which the objects are different shades of the same colour.
- Set up a still life in which the objects are of a similar colour but of different textures.
- Make a still life painting of objects you have chosen one at a time from around the room. Complete one object first, then choose another one and add it to the group and so on - make sure your group is an interesting one!
- Paint a still life of man- made objects only eg toys.
- Paint a still life of natural objects only eg shells.
- Paint a still life of natural and man-made objects

Links with the work of Other Artists

Japanese Paintings
Hundertwasser
Kline
Van Gogh

Materials

Ready Mix or Powder Paint in a dual Primary System ie
2 reds - Crimson and Vermillion
2 blues- Turquoise and Bright blue
2 yellows- Lemon and Brilliant yellow
Black and White
Paint brushes thick and thin
Water pots
Mixing Palettes
FreeArt Paper 80 gsm
Grey sugar paper
Pieces of card 4 sheet thickness

Suppliers

NES Arnold Ltd
Ludlow Hill Road
West Bridgeford
NOTTINGHAM
NG2 6HD

Pisces
Westwood Studies
West Avenue
CREWE
Cheshire
CW1 3AD

Philip & Tracey Ltd
North Way
Andover
Hampshire
SP10 5BA

Hope Education
Orb Mill
Huddersfield Road
OLDHAM
Lancashire
OL4 2ST

Yorkshire Purchasing Organisation
41 Industrial Park
WAKEFIELD
WF2 0XE

Printing

Printing

Session One

Activity Simple Stencils

Focus Shape, Line and Pattern

Equipment Needed

Strong paper or card (waxed card from food packaging is ideal) in strips and whole pieces, chalks or chalk pastels, card on which to create blobs of chalk powder, hair spray as a fixative, scissors, craft knives and cutting mats, wax crayons, FreeArt paper (80gsm) cut to both A4 and A3 size. If stencils were to be used for a print on fabric, sticky backed plastic makes ideal stencils - cut the shapes with the backing still attached and only remove it when you are ready to attach the stencil to the fabric. In this case paint would be needed rather than chalk.

Talk About

• What a stencil is and where children may have seen stencilled patterns.
• Stencil designs on wallpaper borders, fabric borders and furniture.
• The names of different types of stencil, (positive, negative and edge) what they mean and how they are made eg Positive stencils are when a shape is cut out of the centre of a piece of card, and when placed on a paper only the shape can be coloured as the rest of the card masks the outside area. Negative stencils are when a shape is cut from a piece of card, this shape alone is then placed on the paper and coloured over - the shape will remain white whilst the surrounding area becomes coloured. Edge stencils are made by cutting an interesting edge to a piece of card, placing it on a piece of paper adding colour along the edge, then moving it down the paper and adding more colour and so on to create lines of graded colour.
• Drawing simple shapes, without too much detail, to cut out.
• Pressing the stencil down firmly on the paper to prevent colour spreading and spoiling the print.

Sketchbook Work

Look up the word 'stencil' and write down what it means. If you have seen stencils or stencil kits write down where you saw them. Collect pictures of stencil patterns from magazines. When you have made and used your different types of stencils, stick them in your sketchbook. Name each type and how you made them. If you make an extra print from each one you could include them too. Remember to 'fix' them first or they will smudge!

Doing

Choose a strip of card and with a wax crayon draw an interesting line parallel to the longest edge - it could be wavy, zig-zagged etc or keep changing as it is drawn from one side of the card to the other. Use a pair of scissors and cut along your line carefully. You now have a different edge to the top of your card strip - this is your edge stencil. You are going to use chalk pastels with each stencil. Take a piece of card and chalk pastels, choose one colour and make a blob of powder with it on your card. Now place your card strip on a piece of A4 paper. Press it down firmly with one hand and dip a finger of the other hand into the powder and then along the edge of your cut strip of card - make sure you rub upwards each time on to the paper and add the colour as evenly as you can. When you reach the end of your strip, move your stencil and you should have a print of your cut line. Place the strip further down the paper or at a different angle and rub colour upwards from it again - you might like to try another colour. Soon you should have a stencilled pattern of lines. For your negative stencil draw and cut a simple shape (use wax crayon)- a house, a fish or a circle out of a new piece of card. Place it on a piece of A4 paper and fasten it down with blutac, make chalk colour as before and rub it on outwards around the edge of the shape, lift off the stencil to reveal a white shape. Move it to other parts of your paper and repeat. For your positive stencil draw a simple shape with wax crayon in the centre of a new piece of card (leave at Least 4cm around the shape) and cut it out carefully - you may need to use a craft knife. Place it on a new piece of A4 paper, fasten it down with bluetac, make chalk colour as before and rub it inwards in the shape you have cut out, lift off the stencil to reveal a coloured shape. Move it to other parts of your paper and repeat.

Developing the Idea

• Use a line stencil to create a wave pattern or a pattern of mountains.
• Add details to a negative print eg scales to a fish by printing with fingers or cotton wool buds and paint.
• Create a scene using several negative stencils.
• Create a pattern along a line or in a circle using a positive stencil.
• Cut a stencil based on a motif from another culture eg Africa or Egypt

Links with the work of Other Artists

Using the Work of Other Artists
Interior Design Magazines
Ceramics with stencil patterns on them
Wallpaper designs

Printing

Session Two

Activity Borders and Central Motifs

Focus Colour, Shape and Pattern

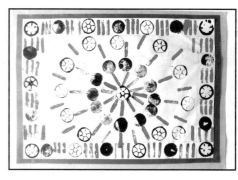

Equipment Needed

Coloured sugar paper or Activity paper cut to A3 size, Assorted junk materials eg lids, boxes, cotton wool buds, draught excluder (for making printing blocks), matchsticks, strips of card etc, paintbrushes, palettes or pieces of card to use as palettes, paper towels, water pots, ready mix paint in either a single or dual primary system plus black and white, scrap pieces of paper that match the coloured paper - on which to try out motifs and colours - and drawing pencils.

Talk About

- What a border pattern is and what a central motif is. Which pattern repeats and which does not, and how they relate to each other in size, shape and colour.
- Border patterns around pages in books, on clothes, scarves, tablecloths, ceramics etc as well as border patterns and central motifs found on objects and textiles from other cultures.
- Where both patterns will be arranged ie the border goes (around the edge) and the central motif needs to be in the middle.
- Making both patterns match in some way though one will be larger than the other.
- Choosing colours and shapes that look good on the background colour.

Sketchbook Work

Describe the difference between a border pattern and a central motif and where each one is arranged in a design. Collect pictures from magazines that show border patterns and central motifs. Draw a large square in your sketchbook and sketch in a border pattern and a central motif of your own - make sure the border pattern repeats as it goes round the square and that it matches the central motif (which appears only once and is larger). The border pattern may be slightly simpler and not have all the shapes of the central motif. Make a list of the printing materials and describe how to make a printing block using a lid and sticky backed draught excluder. When you have tried and chosen colours on a scrap piece of coloured paper this can be added to your sketchbook page. When you have tried printing with different materials and planned a motif this too can be added. You could also make a rough sketch of your finished piece of work.

Doing

Choose a scrap piece of coloured paper that you like, some paint, a brush and a paper towel. On your coloured piece of paper paint several blobs of other colours that you might want to use. Some will look better with the background colour than others. You will only need to use about four in your final pattern or it will become too complicated. Tick the four that you finally decide on. Now choose a piece of white FreeArt paper, some black paint and the items of junk you want to print with - you can add more or change your choice as you try out ideas for a design. Try out some ideas for a central motif first, you may want to explore several ideas and then choose the one you like best. Working in black paint only will help you to see clearly how the shapes look next to each other, around each other, inside and outside each other etc. When you have a design for your central motif you need to choose some but NOT all the shapes you have used to print a border design. It needs to be similar in some way and relate to the central motif. On both your black prints you will need to mark in the colours you have already chosen to use - remember to repeat the same colour for each matching shape. Choose your coloured piece of A3 paper, use your ruler to measure and find the centre and mark it with a dot. To plan where the border will go rule a feint line along each edge about 5 cm in. Get the colours and the junk materials you plan to use and begin to print your central motif. Turn the paper as you work so that you don't smudge your print. Next you will need to choose the shapes and colours for your border pattern. Print along or inside the line you have drawn - remember to stop and turn the corner where the lines cross. Your finished work should show two similar patterns, one that repeats and one that doesn't, with a space between the border pattern and the one in the centre.

Developing The Idea

- Print a border and central pattern using only two colours.
- Print a border and central pattern using only two printing materials.
- Print a border and central pattern using lines only.
- Print a border and central pattern that has a theme eg the sea or flowers-you will probably need to make printing blocks for this as well as using junk.
- Print a border and central design based on a design from another culture eg Paisley patterns.

Links with the work of Other Artists

Scarves and tablecloths and carpets.
Saris with border patterns
Border patterns around pages in books.
Paper plates and matching napkins with border patterns

Printing

Session   Three

Activity   Folded and Symmetrical Prints

Focus   Colour and Shape

Equipment Needed
FreeArt paper (80gsm) or white sugar paper cut to A4 size or slightly smaller, coloured wax crayons, white chalk, paper towels and drawing pencils (4b-6b).

Talk About
• What symmetry means.
• What mirror image means.
• Things that are symmetrical - make a collection of objects and pictures.
• How to fold and label the paper before starting work.
• Working with the paper either landscape or portrait way up.
• Working only on one side of the fold first-using chalk.
• Rubbing the chalk into the grain of the paper with a paper towel or finger and making sure it covers all of one side.
• Knocking off the surplus chalk carefully into a bin or on to a paper towel and not on to the working surface.
• Adding crayon work thickly and carefully and avoiding rubbing the layer of chalk away.
• Refolding the paper before making a drawing.
• Only drawing half a picture - the print will make the other half.

Sketchbook Work
Make a list of things that are symmetrical. Collect pictures from magazines of things that are symmetrical - this might include pictures of reflections in water - and choose some to stick in your sketchbook. Look up the words 'symmetrical' and 'mirror image' and write down what they mean. When you have made your symmetrical print, write down step by step instructions on how to do it. If possible add some diagrams as well. List all the materials that you have used to make your print.

Doing
Choose a piece of white paper and fold it in half. Open it up and in the corner lightly label one half 'A' and the other half 'B'. You are going to work on side 'B' first - at this stage it doesn't matter whether you work with the paper landscape or portrait way up. Take a piece of white chalk and totally cover side 'B' -check that none of it has been missed-then rub the chalk into the paper with either your finger or a paper towel. Now knock off the surplus chalk carefully into the bin or on to a paper towel - NOT on to the work surface or the floor! You are now going to add a thick

layer of wax crayon in patches of different colour-these patches should touch and overlap. If you don't press on firmly and make a thick colouring of wax the print will not be effective. You need to take care not to touch the paper with your crayoning hand whilst you work - if you rub off the chalk layer the print will not work. When your crayoning is complete refold the paper and with a pencil draw a pattern of lines and shapes on the BACK of side A. You will find it easier if the drawing pencil is slightly blunt, a point might make a hole in the paper. Press down firmly as you draw on top of the folded paper. Work from the fold towards the open edges. When you have drawn part of your pattern, open the paper gently to see what is happening. Your pattern will appear on the underside of the paper you are drawing on as well as on side B. Close the paper carefully and continue with your pattern. When it is finished, open the paper fully. Your pattern should now be on both sides of the fold ie on both side A and side B. They will be a mirror image of each other.

Developing the Idea
• Instead of a pattern draw half a face, half an insect, half a leaf, half a house, or half a feather, working along the fold towards the open edges. Work with the paper portrait way up.
• Make a scene reflected in water on the folded paper landscape way up. The scene will need to be drawn upwards from the fold - although in the finished opened print this will actually become the reflection.
• Try working on different colours of paper.
• Try working on different shapes of paper.
• Try working on different sizes of paper.

Links with the work of Other Artists
Masks
Greek Pottery
Charles Rennie Mackintosh

Printing

Session Four

Activity Extending Monoprinting

Focus Colour, Shape and Texture

Equipment Needed
Printing ink (water based) in assorted colours, plastic spoons to put blobs of printing ink on to the wipeable surface or inking trays, rollers, inking trays or a wipeable surface on which to roll out the ink, scissors, scraps of FreeArt paper (80 gsm) and pieces cut to A4 size, tracing paper or kitchen foil, drawing pencils (4b - 6b), masking tape, card pieces as palettes.

Talk About
• What a monoprint is and how to make one - ie putting a blob of printing ink on a wipeable surface and spreading it out with a roller, drawing into the inked surface with a finger or handle of a brush, laying paper on top of the drawing and gently pressing it down to take a print.
• Rolling ink on other surfaces - crumpled foil or tracing paper.
• Using monoprints as a background for a collage, a drawing, painting or adding to it with further printing using junk materials.
• What masking out means.
• Masking out areas with leaves, string or cut out shapes.
• Making random designs or regular repeating arrangements.
• Adding to these masked out shapes later.
• Taking prints on cut out shapes of paper eg a dragon.
• Using several colours of ink to draw a design with a brush before taking a print.

Sketchbook Work
Look up the words 'monoprint' and 'masking out' and write down what they mean. List the tools and materials you are going to use. After you have made several different sorts of monoprint describe how they were done and the one you feel is the most successful. Stick some examples of your prints into your sketch book when they are dry - printing ink will take much longer than paint to dry! Describe how you might use or combine these prints to make a further piece of work.

Doing
Take a piece of foil or greaseproof paper and crumple it into an interesting pattern or texture. Smooth it out, spoon a blob of one colour of printing ink on to it and spread it gently with a roller. Lay a piece of paper on top of the inked surface, press it down gently all over, lift off the paper and you should have a textured monoprint. Take a second print from the same inked surface - this should be more subtle and delicate. For a second type of monoprint cut some pieces of scrap paper into several shapes eg

they could be the same shapes such as triangles in lots of different sizes, or a group of different shapes. Put a blob of one colour printing ink on a palette or wipeable surface and arrange the cut out shapes on it. These will cover and mask areas of the ink so that it wont print and leave plenty of spaces that will. Lay a piece of paper on top of your design and press it down all over it. Make sure you press firmly on the edges of the masked shapes to get a definite outline. Lift off the paper to reveal your print together with white spaces where you lay your cut out shapes. You have made a masked monoprint. You could add to and decorate these white shapes using other media when the ink is dry. For your third monoprint you are going to use several colours of ink and a brush. First get some masking tape and mark out an A4 or slightly smaller space on the wipeable surface - if you work directly onto an inking tray you wont need to mask the edges. Take a card palette and put blobs of all the colours you want to use on it. With a brush paint a picture or a pattern with the ink on your inking tray or inside your masked off space. You will need to work fairly quickly to avoid the ink drying, keep the ink reasonably thick - too thick and there will be blotches of too much strong colour, too thin and it will be faint and dull. Place a piece of paper on top of the finished design and rub it down gently. Lift it off and view the finished print. After taking the first print, add new areas of colour on top and take another print.

Developing the Idea
• Roll ink on to a wipeable surface and make an observational drawing in it of eg a feather or a shell using the handle of a brush. Take a print of it.
• Work on different colours of paper.
• Cut out of silhouettes of buildings, boats or trees for a masked monoprint.
• Use leaves, string or other flat objects to mask out areas before taking a print.
• Cut out shapes of animals or fish, take a monoprint on those shapes and then stick them on a different background - which could be plain, painted or drawn on to create a scene.
• Paint a picture of flowers from observation or imagination on a wipeable surface and take a print - they could be in the style of another artist eg Klimt or Van Gogh

Links with the work of Other Artists
Andy Warhol
John Piper
John Burningham
Brian Wildsmith

Printing

Session   Five

Activity   Further Printing Blocks

Focus   Shape, Pattern and Texture.

Equipment Needed
Thin card both in pieces and cut into squares (12x12 cm) these will be the base of the block, scissors, glue, glue spreaders, wax crayons, corrugated card, textured wallpaper, clay or plasticene, rolling pins, paper towels, plastic knives, printing ink, rollers, inking trays, FreeArt paper cut to A4 size, coloured sugar paper. Drawing pencils (4b-6b).

Talk about
- Making a block of cut out card shapes stuck on a base of card.
- Layering the shapes on top of each other and gluing them down.
- Taking a rubbing of the block using wax crayon.
- Taking a print of the block using roller and printing ink or saving the block as a collage.
- Making several printing shapes from clay or plasticene.
- How to roll out the clay before cutting out the shapes.
- Allowing the shapes, if cut from clay, to dry.
- Inking up the shapes and printing with them.

Sketchbook Work
Cut out several card shapes and glue them within a square shape you have drawn on the page. Take a piece of FreeArt paper and a wax crayon and take a rubbing of these shapes. Try moving the paper into different positions and overlapping the rubbings to explore the effects you can get. Draw another square and again stick cut out card shapes inside it. Stick some smaller cut shapes on top of these shapes and again take a number of rubbings. Cut these rubbings out and stick them next to the rubbing blocks you made in your sketchbook. Take rubbings of corrugated card and textured wallpaper to see the effects they give - record what you have used each time. After you have made and used your clay or plasticene blocks describe how you made them and make a print with each block on your sketchbook page. Later when you have made a finished card block, take a rubbing from it and a print, stick some examples of your work in your book.

Doing
Take a square of card as your base, a piece of card to cut shapes from, a pair of scissors and a drawing pencil. On your piece of card draw an outline shape of eg a figure, an animal, a fish or a building etc. The shape must be smaller

than your card base and fairly simple. Cut the shape out and then cut across it in several places, spread the pieces of the (reassembled) shape on to the card base and push them slightly apart before sticking them down. The spaces will make lines appear on the rubbing. Cut some smaller shapes to stick on top of the first layer - these will add detail e g features to a face, scales to a fish etc. Place a piece of FreeArt paper over your block and with the side of a wax crayon rub across the block. Press more firmly on some parts than others for added interest. Try and rub in the same direction for one print, and in several different directions for another. Try moving the block to make a row of repeat rubbings. Place a new piece of paper over the block and instead of a wax crayon run an inked up roller across the paper for a different effect.

For your second printing block you are going to use plasticene or clay. Roll it flat (not too thin) using a rolling pin and cut out some shapes from it using a plastic knife. You could press eg screws, shells, springs etc into the shapes for added texture and interest. Roller the shapes with printing ink or hold them and press them onto an inked up inking tray. Use the shapes to print a design on a coloured piece of paper. N.B. the textures may need to be re-drawn from time to time as they tend to blur under pressure.

Developing the Idea
- Draw a pattern of different lines with PVA glue on a piece of card, when the glue is dry, cut up the card to make an image for a rubbing block.
- Cut lines in the sides of some of the shapes to be used on a block. Fold back part of the shapes for added interest.
- Use corrugated card or textured wallpaper as the second layer on a rubbing block.
- Make a wheel out of plasticene or clay and stick a pencil through as an axle.
- Press textures on to the outer edge. Wheel it across paper in different directions to create a pattern of different lines (wavy, interweaving, parallel etc).
- Make your initials out of clay or plasticene and print a pattern with them.

Links with the work of Other Artists
Using the Work of Other Artists
Indian printing blocks
William Morris
Pugin

Printing

Session   Six

Activity   Screen Printing

Focus   Shape and Colour

Equipment Needed

Screen Printing Inks, Screens (purchased if possible ready covered with screen printing gauze), masking tape to edge the screen and provide an edge on which to put the ink and rest the squeegee, squeegees, paper for making torn and cut stencils, scissors or a cutting knife and mat, paper (FreeArt 80 gsm) or plain fabric to print on that is slightly larger than the screen itself when it is placed under it. Glue sticks and pieces of coloured sugar paper for sketch book work.

Talk About

• Using a screen, inks and a stencil to create an image.
• Placing a piece of paper under the screen to print on.
• Making a torn paper stencil to lie on the paper.
• Where to put the ink on the screen, how to drag the ink across the screen and the name of the tool to use (a squeegee).
• Working as a group on each print - but getting slightly different results by adding a range of colours (these prints will be negative prints).
• Cutting a stencil in a piece of paper that matches the screen in size.
• The sort of image that it will print (a positive print).
• Washing the screen thoroughly after use.
• The sorts of things that are printed using this method -T-shirts, posters, pictures, etc. In many cases nowadays stencils are applied to the screen by means of photographic techniques.

Sketchbook Work

Make a list of the equipment you are going to use and what each piece is for. Make rough sketches of the equipment to go with your list. Look up the words positive and negative and write down what they mean. Tear some coloured pieces of paper into strips, arrange and stick them on your page as an example of a negative stencil. Cut a shape out of the centre of a coloured piece of paper using scissors or a cutting knife and mat. Stick this on your page as an example of a positive stencil. When you have made a screen print, describe how you did it and whether you feel your design was successful - or how you might improve it. Look for art work by artists that are described as 'screen prints' and write down their titles and the name of the artist who made the print.

Doing

Get into small groups. All the members of the group will be making part of the stencil. Each needs to tear a shape out of paper and arrange it on a large piece of paper, if the screen has a hinge it can be raised and the shapes arranged under it, if not the screen can be put into place on top of the shapes once they have been arranged. Look through the screen mesh, you need to be able to see all the shapes or else they wont be part of the print.They must also be smaller than the screen or they will block out the ink and nothing will print. Spoon the printing ink along the top edge of the screen - decide on the colours as a group,make sure there is sufficient to complete the crossing from one edge of the screen to the other. If you put blobs of several different colours you should get a multicoloured striped print! Initially the stencil needs fixing to the screen. To do this, drag the ink down the screen using a squeegee held at 45 degrees with a single firm, slow movement. Lift off the squeegee and scrape off the excess ink. Raise the screen, the stencil should remain attached to it for further use, and reveal a screen print on the paper below. Each member of the group can make their own print using the same stencil, topping up or adding to the colours, placing their own piece of paper under the screen and dragging the ink across it using a squeegee. Each print should be slightly different. At the end of the session the screen will need washing to remove the colour and the shadow left by the torn stencil.

A cut stencil - each one made individually can be printed in the same way using a shared screen. The paper from which each stencil is cut must be the same size as the frame and the cut out needs to be in the centre. Each member of the group will need to position their own cut stencil under the screen and on top of their paper, to add or top up the ink and use the squeegee to make their print. Wash the screen when all the group have finished.

Developing the Idea

• Tear shapes and print in one colour only, allow the print to dry, tear a new group of shapes and overprint using a different colour.
• Print on different colours of paper.
• Mix printing inks together for interesting blends to print with.
• Cut eg a leaf shape out of a piece of paper and make a print, add detail by drawing when the print has dried. If the print was made on to fabric, detail could be in the form of stitching and embellishment with sequins etc.
• Each group member cut out a flower design -each design in turn is printed on the same piece of paper or fabric.

Links with the work of Other Artists

Andy Warhol
Screen Printed Fabrics
Sonia Delauney

Materials

Card
Chalks or chalk pastels
Hair Spray
Reclaimed Materials
Cotton wool buds, Matchsticks
Paintbrushes
Paint
Palettes or Inking Trays
Coloured paper
FreeArt paper 80gsm
Wax crayons and drawing pencils 4b-6b
Masking tape
Printing ink and rollers
Corrugated card,textured wallpaper
Plasticene,clay
Glue, glue spreaders
Screens, squeegees, printing ink
Plain fabric

Suppliers

NES Arnold Ltd
Ludlow Hill Road
West Bridgeford
NOTTINGHAM
NG2 6HD

Pisces
Westwood Studies
West Avenue
CREWE
Cheshire
CW1 3AD

Philip & Tracey Ltd
North Way
Andover
Hampshire
SP10 5BA

Hope Education
Orb Mill
Huddersfield Road
OLDHAM
Lancashire
OL4 2ST

Yorkshire Purchasing Organisation
41 Industrial Park
WAKEFIELD
WF2 0XE

Printing

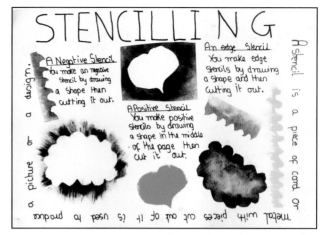

Session 2
Example of borders and central motif.

Session 3
Example of folded and symmetrical print.

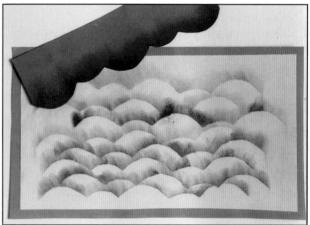

Session 1
Examples of simple stencils.

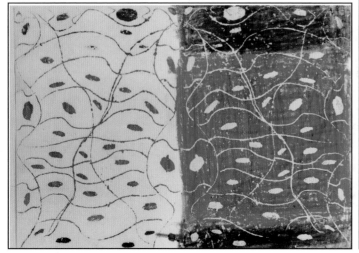

Printing

Session 4 -
Example of extended monoprinting.

Session 6 - Example of screen printing.

Session 5
Example of further
printing blocks.

34

Collage

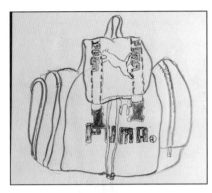

Session 2
Examples of working from observation (1st hand).

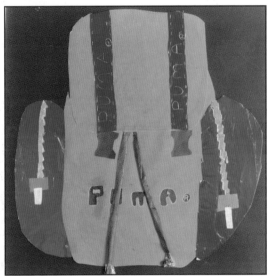

Session 1
Example of working from observation (2nd hand).

Session 3
Example of abstracting from a source.

Collage

Session 6
Example of a mixed media decorative collage.

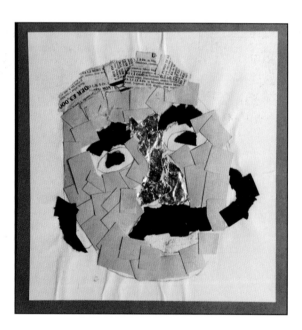

Session 5
Examples of torn images.

Session 4
Examples of developing a design.

Collage

Collage

Session   One

Activity   Working from Observation (2nd hand)

Focus   Colour, Shape, Pattern and Texture

Equipment Needed
Portraits of famous people from History eg Henry VIII, his wives, Elizabeth I, Mary Queen of Scots etc (head and shoulders only if possible rather than a full length portrait).Coloured magazines, scissors, glue, glue spreaders, FreeArt paper (80 gsm) cut to A4 size or slightly larger. Drawing pencils (4b-6b) and wax or pencil crayon for sketchbook work.

Talk About
• The people in the portraits, who they were, what they did and why they were famous.
• Who painted the portraits
• Who might have asked for them to be painted.
• Why the portraits might in fact flatter the sitter rather than be a true likeness - so the artist got paid!
• Where these portraits would have been hung - and can be seen today.
• The colours used by the artist.
• The pose and expression of the subject.
• The clothes and jewels they are wearing and the background setting - all of which convey wealth and importance.
• Why there are few pictures of working people or servants.
• Why this is second hand observation - work is done from a picture or photograph instead of an actual object, building, person or landscape etc.

Sketchbook Work
Stick in a photocopy of your favourite portrait, describe it and say why you like it. Stick in a photocopy of your least favourite portrait, describe it and say why you don't like it. Find out details of the subjects of both portraits and the artists in each case. Choose a portrait to copy and describe that. List the clothes the sitter is wearing - the colour and texture of the fabrics - hats or headresses and jewellery. Describe their expression, whether they are holding anything and what the setting is like in which the subject is placed. Make a list of all the colours you can see and will have to match. Try making a sample of each of the colours using either wax crayons or pencil crayons or both.

Doing
Put the portrait you are going to work from at the top of your piece of FreeArt paper (portrait way up). Look carefully at the space above the head, at either side of the head, and how the neck and shoulders fill the space below. Your portrait will need to match this use of space. Draw the outline of the face with your fingers on your paper to get an idea of the space you will need for it. Now lightly draw in pencil the outline ONLY of the face - you are going to add all the details in collage. Collect some coloured magazines and look through them for a pair of eyes that are similar in size and shape to those in your portrait, cut them out carefully. You now need to look for a match for all the other features - nose, ears, mouth etc. When you have collected the features you need, build up the face shape with overlapping torn pieces from magazines - match the colour as carefully as you can. Glue the pieces down, then add the features you collected. You may need to add hair next - this might be torn or cut pieces of pictures that match the colour and texture in the portrait. Pictures of soil, fabric, tree branches which are the unexpected are worth looking at as well as pictures of actual hair. Continue adding to your portrait - clothes, jewels etc - matching colours, shapes and textures as carefully as you can in torn and cut overlapping pieces. As you look for a match remember you might find what you need in an unexpected setting eg a picture of a garden rather than in a picture of people. Display the finished portraits alongside those that have been observed.

Developing the Idea
• Make your own self -portrait from a photograph of your self.
• Make a collage portrait from a self portrait painted by an artist - Van Gogh did several.
• Make a collage portrait from a picture of a pop star or a sports star.
• Make a collage portrait from a portrait you have drawn of yourself or a friend.

Links with the work of Other Artists
Holbein
Nicholas Hilliard
Gainsborough

Collage

Session   Two

Activity   Working From Observation
(1st hand)

Focus   Colour, Shape and Pattern

Equipment Needed
FreeArt paper (80 gsm) cut to A3 size as background material, Sugar paper in assorted colours cut to A3 size, scissors, glue, glue spreaders, drawing pencils (4b-6b), chalk, coloured foil and black paper A4 size. Stimulus material from which to work - Sports bags, or multicoloured trainers are ideal for this session. Black felt tip pens or handwriting pens for sketchbook work.

Talk About
• The difference between second hand observation in the previous session, and first hand observation in this - ie when the actual stimulus material is there to be touched, rearranged and viewed from a variety of angles.
• The object you are looking at - describe what it is, its purpose etc.
• The large shapes that make up the object to be worked ·from.
• The small shapes that make up the object to be worked from.
• The position of these shapes and how they fit together.
• How these shapes convey eg the sides, top, front etc of the object.
• The patterns, lettering or details on the object.
• Working on the largest shape first and attaching the other shapes to it.
• Arranging all the shapes together without gluing them until you are satisfied.
• Adding the details last.

Sketchbook Work
Describe the object you are going to work from and make a rough outline sketch of it. You may want to sketch it from several viewpoints before you have the sketch you want to use. Use a black felt tip or handwriting pen to divide your chosen sketch of the object into simple shapes. Make a list and individual sketches of each shape in turn. Practice copying the lettering, if any, on your object. Look at the size and style of the lettering carefully. Make a collection of other logos for different products to stick on your page. Add pictures of other types of objects eg sports bags that are slightly different from the one you are working from. Describe your own sports bag - or one you would like to own and say why. Describe the difference between first hand and second hand observation.

Doing
Look carefully at the object in front of you, and the A3 paper on which it must fit as a collage. Feel the outline of the different shapes that make up your object, with your finger. Find the piece of coloured sugar paper that most closely matches your object in colour. LIGHTLY sketch on it with a drawing pencil or chalk the largest shape you can see. Cut it out carefully and place it on your piece of background paper. Now sketch the smaller shapes that fit next to the large shape. Cut them out carefully and arrange them on the background. Continue drawing cutting and arranging the shapes until you have assembled the complete object on your page. Look at all the shapes together, do they make up the shape you observed? Are any too large or too small? Do you need to change any of them? If so you can do it now and then when you are satisfied, glue the shapes down on to your background paper. You now need to draw and cut out any details eg stitching, eyelets, pockets, handles, lettering etc and add them to your collage. You have made an observational drawing but in collage. Display the objects and the collages together. The collage shapes may look more effective if they are cut round and re- mounted on a new background before they are displayed - a neutral colour will be best.

Developing the Idea
• Make an observational collage of an object of your own choosing.
• Make a collage of a new type of sports bag - some of the shapes may be similar but others may be different.
• Make a collage of a new type of trainer - complete with logo.
• Make a collage of a matching T-shirt - complete with logo.
• Make a collage of a personalised trainer or a personalised sports bag for yourself.
• Make an observational collage of a group of objects.

Links with the work of Other Artists
Peter Blake
Kurt Schwitters
Graham Sutherland

Collage

Session   Three

Activity   Abstracting from a Source

Focus   Shape, Line and Pattern

Equipment Needed

Viewfinders, drawing pencils (4b-6b), grey sugar paper cut to A3 size as a background, pieces of black and white paper and silver foil (A3 and A4) to cut up, glue, scissors, a guitar as stimulus material - it is large, easily observed and offers a variety of possible shapes to abstract.

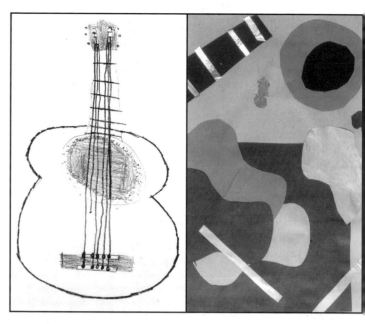

Talk About

• What the word abstract means and what an abstract picture is - a series of lines, shapes and colours taken and developed from a stimulus eg an object, an emotion, a piece of music, a view etc and arranged in a new and interesting way.

• How an abstract picture is different from a figurative picture - a picture that closely resembles the stimulus that has been observed.

• Sorting postcard pictures showing the work of different artists into groups - those that are abstract and those that are figurative.

• The different shapes on a guitar, large, small, thick, thin, similar, flat, curved etc also the centre hole, the pegs and strings.

• The need to use the different shapes individually and not connected as they are on the actual guitar. Some of the shapes may touch or overlap in the new arrangement. They may have cut outs made in them or shapes added on top of them for interest. Some shapes might appear cut in half, and shapes may appear more than once but the paper used may be different.

• The work will be monochrome ie black, white, grey and silver - not coloured.

Sketchbook Work

Look up the word 'abstract' and record what it means. Find two artists' pictures that are abstract, write down the names of the artists and the titles of their work. Look up the word 'figurative' and record what it means. Find two artists pictures that are figurative, write down the names of the artists and the titles of their work. Look up the word 'monochrome', and record what it means. Stick pieces of the monochrome collage materials that are available on your page. Use a viewfinder to look at different parts of the guitar - it will help you discover lots of interesting shapes. Now without using the viewfinder look at the shapes again and sketch the outlines of different ones - don't add too much detail yet, you can do that in your collage. You will need to sketch plenty of shapes to have a choice for your final piece of work.

Doing

Take a piece of A3 grey paper as your background, some scissors and pieces of black, white and silver paper. Look at the shapes you have drawn in your sketch book and choose one to draw (lightly) and cut out. You need to decide which type of paper you are going to cut it from and the size it is going to be. When you have cut out your shape, lay it on your background paper and begin work on a second one. Again you will need to consider its size and the paper it is going to be cut from. Continue until you have several shapes. Try arranging them in different ways on the background, look at the spaces between them - gaps are important too and can add interest and focus. Are any of the shapes too large, too small, or too similar in size? Do any need shapes cutting out of them? Could any be cut in half and the two halves slightly separated? Remember it is not meant to look like the actual guitar but based on it. When you are happy with your arrangement, glue it down. You are now ready to add detail to some of the shapes, to add smaller shapes on top or an outlines next to some of them. Look carefully at how much and where you use each of the different papers. Everyone's finished abstracts should show interesting arrangements of similar shapes. Display the collages as a block arrangement with the guitar in front.

Developing the Idea

• Select your own object to make an abstract collage from.

• Make an abstract collage based on a group of objects.

• Make an abstract collage using coloured papers that match the stimulus material.

• Make a 3D collage by attaching eg the guitar shapes to the different surfaces on the lid of a box. Allow some of the shapes to stick out and extend beyond the box.

Links with the work of Other Artists

Terry Frost
Gillian Ayres
Howard Hodgkin

Collage

Session   Four

Activity   Developing a Design

Focus   Line, Shape and Pattern

Equipment Needed

Drawing pencils (4b-6b), FreeArt Paper 80 gsm cut to A3 and A4 size for a background, pieces of grey and black sugar paper and silver foil plus strips of each colour for folding and producing repeat patterns. Coloured papers cut to A3 and A4 as background for developing the work plus pieces and strips of coloured paper and foil to cut up, scissors, glue, stimulus material eg flowers or plants are a good starting point for this work, examples of pattern work made up of flowers - wrapping paper and William Morris designs will offer plenty of different arrangements.

Talk About

- The different shapes of the flower heads and leaves to be sketched from observation.
- Choosing the flower shapes and drawing them on the BACK of coloured paper before cutting them out -to avoid pencil marks on the finished collage.
- Folding a piece of paper to cut out more than one of the same flower type. Folding a strip in half (twice) drawing a flower shape on the folded strip, cutting it out leaving a join to the piece behind at each edge, opening the strip for a line of repeated shapes.
- The way these flower shapes are arranged, how they repeat and form a pattern both on the wrapping paper and the William Morris designs.
- The different sizes and shapes of the flowers and the way that the individual flower shapes link up and overlap with stems, tendrils and leaves.
- How the flower heads and leaves are decorated with lines and shapes.
- The colours used in the designs.
- Working in monochrome - black, white, grey and silver, to start with.

Sketchbook Work

Collect pictures from magazines that show patterns using flowers - examples of wallpaper and furnishing fabrics will offer plenty. Stick some of them on your page and describe your favourite one and why you like it. Look in the library for information about William Morris and record some details about him on your page. Use a drawing pencil and make separate rough outline sketches - like a silhouette - of the shapes of individual leaves and flowers that you see in front of you. You can add details later when you re-draw them. Cut them out and make your finished collage.

Doing

Take a piece of A4 or A3 paper to use as a background and some pieces of grey, black and silver to cut up and use for your flower and leaf shapes. Look at the sketches you have already made of flowers and leaves and decide which one you want to use first. It will probably be easier to cut out and arrange flower heads only to begin with and to add stems and leaves later - unless your design is going to be made up of leaves alone. You need to choose the sort of paper you are going to draw them on, how big they are going to be and how many you need of each (do you need to fold the paper?)You might want to do a joined up row of flowers between individual flower heads. There are lots of possibilities for you to try. If you cut and arrange your shapes before using glue you can move them around until you are happy with the design, and then stick them down. Continue adding to your design using all the papers available, linking the shapes together but also leaving spaces for interest. Look at the William Morris designs for ideas of arrangement and repetition. Finally you could add detail to some of the petals, stems and leaves using contrasting papers, cut lines and small shapes. Each similar flower or leaf will need to be decorated in the same way. Your monochrome collage should show an interesting design that you could imagine being on a textile, greetings card or wallpaper.

Developing the Idea

- Choose a coloured background and cut out the same shapes as in your monochrome collage. Use three or four colours that look good on your background colour and arrange the cut shapes in the same way as before.
- Display the two designs side by side - which do you prefer and why?
- Develop a design based on man-made objects eg keys of different sizes and shapes.
- Develop a design for a purpose eg to decorate a beach towel or a bath towel. Sketch appropriate motifs before you start.
- Develop a design based on a motif from another culture eg a paisley shape.

Links with the work of Other Artists

Using the Work of Other Artists
Laura Ashley Wallpaper
Wrapping paper
Art Nouveau

Collage

Session Five

Activity Torn Images

Focus Shape, Colour, Pattern and Texture

Equipment Needed

Different types of papers eg sugar paper, tissue, cellophane, brown paper, gift wrap, wallpaper, corrugated paper, foil, unwanted marbling, painting or printing, newspapers and magazines. Glue, glue spreaders, FreeArt paper 80gsm cut to both A3 and A4 size to offer a choice of background, drawing pencils (4b-6b) and pieces of black paper for sketch book work. Newspaper and magazine pictures of faces including portraits by various artists and illustrations of masks.

Talk About

- The different sorts of paper available and what they are all called.
- Tearing small shapes, strips, curves, circles, zig-zags etc out of paper and tearing the paper without drawing on it first. NOT tearing an actual face shape to start with but just arranging and combining features to form a face.
- Looking at the main features that could be torn.
- Arranging shapes before sticking them down.
- Adding detail to a shape by tearing and adding further pieces on top of it.
- Combining a range of colours shapes and textures to add interest and create impact.
- Giving the face an expression eg surprise, sadness etc by experimenting with different torn shapes.
- That this is is not an actual face or portrait but an imaginative approach to one.

Sketchbook Work

Stick snippets of all the papers available on your page and write next to each one the type of paper that it is. Make a collection of faces cut from magazines that show different expressions. Stick your favourites in your book. Record the titles of your portraits by other artists that you like, the names of the artists and a little bit about them. Practice drawing eye shapes and then tearing different eye shapes out of a black piece of paper. Do the same with all the other main features eg ears, nose, mouth etc. From each group of torn features you need to choose one to use in your final portrait. Use a drawing pencil to sketch out and combine the chosen features to make a face. You may want to sketch several arrangements before you have one you want to work from.

Doing

Choose your background paper, place it portrait way up, and after looking carefully at the face you have sketched in your book collect a range of different papers for the features you are going to tear. To add interest to your portrait you will need to consider the choice of colours, patterns and textures carefully. They need to look good together and add interest but not clash or distract from the work. You may need to change your mind, add to or reject papers whilst you work. Remember the features you tear will be of different sizes and need to relate to one another. Start with the nose, tear and place it on the paper first then tear and build up the other features above, below and next to it. Arrange all the features before sticking them down - it will allow you to change your mind! Don't tear an outline for your face, the arrangement of the features should suggest it is there. Leave the background white to show off your colourful and interesting imaginative torn portrait.

Developing the Idea

- Make a torn paper collage of a character or an event from a story or poem.
- Make a torn paper collage of a figure or several figures moving across the paper - add the limbs to the main body shapes to give the feeling of movement eg running, jumping etc.
- Make a torn paper collage based on an artists work eg Monet's bridge over the waterlily pond or a Picasso portrait.
- Make a torn paper landscape from a sketch you have made or from a photograph.
- Make a torn paper collage of a wild animal or a bird in its natural setting.

Links with the work of Other Artists

Keith Haring
Picasso
African Masks
North American Indian Masks/Totem Poles

Collage

Session   Six

Activity   Mixed Media Decorative Collage

Focus   Colour, Shape, Pattern, Line
and Texture.

Equipment Needed

A collection of found objects eg Buttons, beads, fabric, twigs, bark, wood off-cuts, string, pebbles, plastic netting, corrugated card, bubble wrap, straws, matchsticks, pegs, shells, buttons, feathers, cogs etc, glue, glue spreaders, scissors, double sided tape, a cool melt glue gun to secure heavy items, cardboard boxes to decorate, FreeArt paper (80gsm) to cover the boxes first, ready mix paint to colour them, paint brushes, drawing pencils (4b-6b).

Talk About

• The range of materials to be selected from and worked with.
• The different shapes, colours and textures that can be seen.
• Those that are man-made materials and those that are natural.
• Light materials that can be stuck down with glue.
• The materials that need double sided tape to stick them down eg netting.
• Heavy materials that need to be stuck using a cool melt glue gun.
• How and what to be careful of when using a glue gun.
• The different surfaces of a box that can be decorated and those left alone.
• Covering the box with paper to offer a blank surface for decoration.
• Painting the surface before starting the collage.
• Trying different arrangements on a piece of card before sticking it down on the box itself.
• Themes for a box eg a shiny box, a textured box, a fishy box, a box of round things, a hot box, a cold box, a four seasons box, a birthday box, a box of patterns, a patchwork box, etcList all the class suggestions.
• The finished collages on the boxes will be in low - relief ie they stand up from the surface and are not totally flat.

Sketchbook Work

Write down a description low-relief and what it means. Make a list of all the materials that are available to work with. List the different ways of sticking them down. Describe how to use a low melt glue gun safely. Write down all the ideas suggested by the class as possible themes - add more ideas of your own if you have some. Put a circle around one or two that you might like to try.

List ideas and materials that match your theme. Draw the outline of a box shape on your page and draw on it some of your ideas and arrangements for each surface - they will all need to link to your theme.

Doing

Choose your box to be decorated and cover it in white FreeArt paper. Decide what colour you want it to be, get some paint and a brush and paint it- you might want all the sides the same colour or each side to be a different colour or a different shade of one colour. If you want to add some patterns in paint to it before you begin your collage. Keep your sketchbook next to you whilst you work, to remind you of your plan for your box - you may alter it as you work, write about the alterations you made in your sketchbook once your box collage is complete. Begin decorating your box once the paint is dry - collect the materials you plan to use and arrange them to fit on one side of the box, fasten them down and allow the glue to set before working on another side of the box. Each side needs to link to the others and the theme you have chosen - some materials might be arranged in groups, in a circle, in a line or as a border to a central design. If you think carefully as you select and arrange your collage materials your box collage will be attractive and interesting - too much and it will look messy and cluttered.

Developing the Idea

• Decorate a box for a character from a story.
• Decorate a box for a specific person eg a dentist, a musician, a gardener, a cat lover etc
• Decorate a box for a specific artist eg Henry Moore, Jackson Pollock etc
• Decorate a box in response to a piece of music.
• Decorate a box by adding and changing its shape as well as decorating it.

Links with the work of Other Artists

Faberge Easter Eggs
Gift Boxes and Packaging
Jewellery Boxes

Materials

Scissors
Glue, glue spreaders
Drawing pencils 4b-6b
Wax crayons
Coloured sugar paper, black paper, foil
Black felt tip pens
Buttons, beads, fabric, twigs, straws, matchsticks
Netting, corrugated card, bubble wrap
Feathers, shells, cogs
Double sided sellotape, cool melt glue gun
paint, paint brushes

Suppliers

NES Arnold Ltd
Ludlow Hill Road
West Bridgeford
NOTTINGHAM
NG2 6HD

Pisces
Westwood Studies
West Avenue
CREWE
Cheshire
CW1 3AD

Philip & Tracey Ltd
North Way
Andover
Hampshire
SP10 5BA

Hope Education
Orb Mill
Huddersfield Road
OLDHAM
Lancashire
OL4 2ST

Yorkshire Purchasing Organisation
41 Industrial Park
WAKEFIELD
WF2 0XE

Sculpture

Sculpture

Session   One

Activity   Using Other Artists 2D Images as a Starting Point

Focus   Line, Shape, Colour, Pattern and Texture.

Equipment Needed

Pictures of room interiors painted by other artists eg Van Gogh's bedroom at Arles, viewfinders, drawing pencils (4b-6b), wax crayons, paint, brushes, glue, glue spreaders, masking tape, brown matt gummed tape, pieces of card cut to A3 size as the base on which the work will be built, assorted reclaimed materials-boxes, tubes, lids etc, pieces of card, scissors, textiles, yarns, paper of different sorts, matchsticks, art straws, wire, modroc etc, FreeArt paper 80 gsm for covering parts of the construction before adding decoration.

Talk About

- What can be seen as the background in a picture of the interior of a room- wallcoverings, pictures etc including views outside that can be glimpsed through windows-window frames, sills, curtains etc.
- What can be seen covering the floor - floorboards, carpets, tiles, rugs etc
- What furniture is in the room, the different sizes of furniture and how it is arranged.
- What stands on the furniture - vases, mirrors, books etc.
- Using viewfinders to focus on one bit at a time.
- Making the room setting on a card base.
- Making the furniture etc from the materials available- and the range of materials on offer.
- Different ways of joining the materials together.
- Matching the colours, patterns and textures seen as closely as possible by painting and printing and covering the items made for the room.

Sketchbook Work

Write down the titles of some of the pictures of interiors you have looked at, including your favourite and least favourite. Choose one you are going to turn into a 3D construction. Write down and sketch what is on the walls and the floor of the room. Explore making and matching the colours you need for these using wax crayon. Now list the furniture you can see - make a note of the different sizes of the pieces and the different shapes, write down what you might choose to make them from - you may change your mind as you are actually making, write the changes down in your sketch book at the end. Look at things you will need to make that stand on top of the furniture, sketch them and how they might be made as well. Describe your finished room and the parts of it that are least and the most successful.

Doing

You will need to work with your sketches and the picture of the room near to you. Choose your piece of A3 card as the base and colour and decorate it to match the one in your picture. Find some pieces of card to make the walls, remember you need to make them stand up on your base, cut out any windows and decorate the walls, add pictures etc before you attach them to the base. Now you are ready to make the furniture, start with the largest piece, look at where it must stand and how much space it takes up before choosing the materials to make it from. Make all the pieces of furniture in turn and try standing them in the room next to each other before you decorate them - you may need to alter or remake a piece to get the room just right! When all the pieces are made they will need covering, decorating and adding to eg before they are fastened into place. Finally you will need to consider things that stand or are placed on the pieces of furniture. These will be quite small and again you will need to try them on the furniture before you fasten them down. Stand the picture you have worked from next to your finished room to see the 3D match to a 2D image. Display the two together.

Developing the Idea

- Make a 3D model of a room setting in a magazine picture.
- Make a 3D model of a room setting from a picture of a room in another country eg a Mediterranean style room, a Mexican style room.
- Make a 3D model of your own bedroom.
- Make a 3D model of a room of the future.
- Make a 3D model of a room you would like to have.
- Make a model of a room linked to History eg a Victorian parlour.

Links with the work of Other Artists

Bonnard
Matisse
David Hockney
Van Gogh

Sculpture

Session Two

Activity Observational Work on Clay Tiles

Focus Line, Shape and Pattern

Equipment Needed

Vegetables cut in half eg peppers, red cabbage, tomatoes etc with an interesting inner structure to use as a stimulus, viewfinders, drawing pencils (4b-6b), clay, rolling pins, rolling guides or old wooden rulers to ensure the rolled clay tiles are of even thickness, slip ie a runny mixture of clay and water to act as glue for joining pieces on to the clay tile, margarine tubs, lolly sticks, plastic knives and other clay tools for shaping and modelling the clay, paper towels to rest the clay tiles on whilst working, a damp sponge to keep fingers moist whist working. FreeArt paper (80gsm) cut into squares 24x24 cm.

Talk About

- Using a viewfinder to select an interesting part of a vegetable.
- Drawing that part and copying the drawing in low relief on a clay tile.
- How to roll clay to an even thickness using a rolling pin and rolling guides.
- Cutting the rolled clay into a square shaped tile using a plastic knife.
- How slip is made and what it is for.
- Scratching the base of the shapes to be joined to the tile for extra grip before using slip.
- Rubbing slip on with a finger.
- Pinching, carving and pulling some shapes from the surface of the tile itself as well as joining pieces on.
- Looking at the drawing whilst working to match the shapes, patterns and textures recorded.

Sketchbook Work

Make a list of what you need to do before you use the clay- and also how to roll out clay and make a tile shape. Describe slip, how it is made and what it is used for. Describe the vegetable section you have chosen to draw, put your viewfinder on it and make several different rough sketches of different views using a drawing pencil. Draw square shapes on your page to make your sketches in before you start. Look especially at the lines, shapes and patterns in the vegetable section. One of your views might be of the centre of the section, another of part of the edge and part of the inside.Try and make each one different so that you have a choice as to which one to develop further. Don't add too much detail as you are going to turn your sketch into a piece of clay work.

Doing

Work with your sketch book open next to you and on a square piece of paper (24x24cm) make an enlarged drawing of one of the sketches of a vegetable section in your sketch book. This will be the stimulus for your clay work. Take a paper towel and place a lump of clay on it, put rolling guides either side of the clay - a little way from it- and with a rolling pin roll and flatten the clay. When the rolling pin touches both of the rolling guides together the clay will be of equal thickness. Cut out a square tile shape 24x24 cm to match your drawing. If you have chosen a lump of clay that is too small when it is rolled out, roll it back into a ball, add some more and roll that into your ball before you try making a tile again. Make some slip in a margarine tub by adding a little water to a piece of clay and stirring it together until it becomes runny - this is your glue. Look at your drawing and decide where the shapes you have drawn will fit on your tile, which ones you will need to make and add on and which ones you will make out of the tile itself - you could draw outlines lightly on the tile with a plastic knife before you start. Remember to get extra clay and model the shapes you want to join on. Scratch the base of each one and fix them to the tile with slip smeared on with a finger. Your finished tile should look like a low relief copy of your drawing.

Developing the Idea

- The vegetable section could be painted in the colours observed on the original, colour mixing and matching would be needed on paper first. The tiles will paint better if they are first given a coat of a pva and water mix - about half and half - as clay is very porous. Use ready mix or powder paint.
- Make an observed tile of part of a flower head, a leaf or a fruit.
- Make an observed tile of part of an insect or a fish.

Links with the work of Other Artists

Claus Oldenburg
Picasso
Andy Warhol

Sculpture

Session Three

Activity Adding and Padding

Focus Line, Shape, Texture and Form

Equipment Needed

Newspaper, tissue paper in assorted colours, paste and a bowl to make and keep it in or marvin, glue spreaders, strong card cut into 20cm squares to use as a base, masking tape scissors, drawing pencils (4b-6b), ready mix paint, brushes, card palettes - for extension work plastic bottles or silver foil and further pieces of strong card. Pieces of textured bark, pictures of scales on fish and reptiles, pictures of ripples on water to use as a stimulus.

Talk About

• Making parcels of varying size out of newspaper and fastening them together with masking tape. Folding newspaper into strips and curving and bending those strips. Crumpling and creasing pieces of newspaper to make interesting patterns and textures.

• Fastening the parcels, strips and crumpled paper on to a card base using tape or glue, taking care not to flatten and destroy the shapes, patterns and textures.

• Adding shapes and building on to parts of the first layer.

• Tearing newspaper or tissue paper into strips, covering the strips with glue or paste (one strip at a time) and laying them on the padded base to cover all the original shapes but without flattening or squashing them.

N.B. If newspaper and paste is used it will take several days to dry out - it could then be painted - tissue and marvin will make a hard surface which is already coloured but will still need time to dry. Further patterns could be added using a paint and marvin mixture to help the paint cling to the shiny surface.

Sketchbook Work

Collect pictures of tree bark, ripples in water and scales on fish and reptiles to stick in your book. Draw some squares on your page and using one of your pictures as a stimulus, copy in pencil the linear pattern you see in one of your squares. Choose another picture to work from and copy the pattern from that into another square. Continue until you have several different patterns to choose from for your final work. You are going to build one in relief on a card base. Describe how you made it, the way you used the newspaper and tissue to create your structure, after the work is complete.

Doing

Get a square of card, some newspaper and masking tape and your chosen drawn pattern. Look at it carefully to help you decide how you are going to make and arrange it on the card base. Explore making shapes and patterns in different ways with the newspaper, arranging them differently, building up areas, crumpling and folding others until the work looks interesting and varied in height and texture. Fasten the shapes down using tape or glue or both - take care not to squash or flatten them! You are now ready to cover the construction and make it solid. For this you need to tear tissue paper or newspaper into strips, coat one strip at a time in paste or marvin and lay it on your construction. Try not to flatten the shapes - you might even be able to pinch and crease the glued layer as you put it in place to create further patterns and textures. Allow your construction to dry before adding further colour or patterns in paint. Display all the squares together to make a large and interesting textured piece of work. If colour was limited for decoration eg black and white, shades of red etc the final display would be even more striking.

Developing the Idea

• Make a magic wall mirror by adding and padding to a piece of card with a foil piece stuck on as the mirror.

• Make a magic hand mirror with an interesting shape and a handle. Again use foil for the mirror but this time decorate both the front and the back of the card - in turn!

• Add and pad on to a plastic bottle to change it into an unusual shaped bottle.

• Add and pad a bottle to change it into something new eg a jug with a handle, a large candlestick or vase.

• Add and pad a bottle to become a figure, a fish an insect or an animal.

Links with the work of Other Artists

Henry Moore
Gaudi
Barbara Hepworth

Sculpture

Session   Four

Activity   Further Work With Newspaper

Focus   Shape and Form

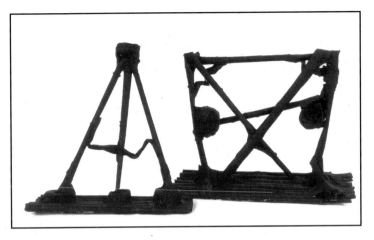

Equipment Needed

Newspaper, masking tape or brown gummed tape (the non shiny variety) drawing pencils (4b-6b). Pictures of interesting buildings, pylons, bridges, scaffolding and sculpture as stimulus material. Modroc to cover the finished constructions - Only if required! - and paint to add colour to the modroc when it is dry. Wet Modroc can be effectively coloured by sprinkling it with dry powdered Brusho or Easibrush dye.

Talk About

- Rolling a page of newspaper tightly to make it into a straw.
- Fastening the newspaper straw at both ends with tape to keep it intact.
- The change in the rigidity of the newspaper now that it has been rolled.
- Bending and joining a group of newspaper straws to build with them.
- The need for a firm base of straws to support the structure.
- Discovering other ways of making newspaper rigid so that it becomes a construction material.
- Folding a page over and over to make a flattened strip, coiling the strip round on itself to form a spiral, securing the end of the spiral to the coil with tape.
- Fastening several spirals together or grouping them inside a circle made from a folded page to make a solid platform or base for a construction.
- Plaiting three strips each made from a folded page and taping each end of the plait before bending it or curling it and building with it.

Sketchbook Work

Describe and draw diagrams, with a drawing pencil, on how to make a newspaper straw, a newspaper spiral and a newspaper plait. Write about the feel of the new shapes, and how they can bent and made into further shapes. Draw some of the shapes you managed to make with a plait or a straw. After you have made a construction using lots of shapes made in different ways from newspaper, draw what you have built. Look for pictures of unusual shaped buildings, scaffolding, pylons, bridges and sculpture to stick in your book, these are for ideas of shapes that fit together in different ways - you are not going to copy and try to make any of them, just to use them for ideas.

Doing

Get some masking tape and plenty of newspaper. You will need to make lots of building material with the newspaper before you begin joining it together to make a construction - you don't have to use it all! Start by making lots of straws, then lots of spirals and several plaits. If you have any new ideas of your own then make them too and record your new ideas in your sketchbook. Remember to tape the ends of the shapes you make or they will begin to unravel! Look at the pictures of bridges etc for ideas and then begin joining your shapes together. The construction you make needs to be interesting to look at from all angles - shapes on top of shapes, shapes under shapes, large shapes, small shapes, thick shapes, thin shapes, groups of similar shapes, groups of different shapes etc - and to be rigid and able to stand on its own. Make extra newspaper shapes, if you need them, as your construction grows. If you want to cover it with modroc and paint it, it will need to be VERY firm. Try not to get it too wet if you cover it, as it will soon become soggy and collapse! Painting will need to be done after the modroc has dried.

Developing the Idea

- Make a construction using newspaper straws only.
- Make a construction using spirals only.
- Make a construction using plaits only.
- Make a construction based on a spiral shell or a piece of coral.
- Make a construction based on a root or twig shape.
- Make a construction that could be worn on your head.

Links with the work of Other Artists

Mackintosh
Gaudi
Hundertwasse

Sculpture

Session   Five

Activity   More Slotted Structures

Focus   Shape, Form and Colour

Equipment Needed
Black card (4 sheet thickness) cut to A4 size, scissors, drawing pencils (4b-6b) white card A3 size, preferably slightly thicker than 4 sheet as it is to be painted, paint, card palettes, brushes. Photographs of unusual shaped buildings eg Sydney Opera house and abstract paintings by Wassily Kandinsky

Talk About
• The different shapes seen on the buildings in the pictures and how those shapes are arranged and fit together.
• Cutting different shapes from pieces of card eg curves, circles, strips etc.
• Cutting slits in some of the shapes to slot and join them on to others.
• The need for a firm base in order that the slotted structure will stand upright.
• The sort of shapes that slot together to make a firm base - and how they slot together.
• Re- arranging the same shapes in several ways on top of the base to create new and different slotted structures.
• The artist Wassily Kandinsky and his work.
• The shapes and colours in the abstract paintings by Kandinsky.
• Cutting similar shapes from white card and slotting them together.
• Painting the shapes before slotting them together.
• Matching the colours to those used by Kandinsky.

Sketchbook Work
Look up the word 'abstract' and write down what it means. Find out some details about Wassily Kandinsky and the titles of some his paintings. Describe the shapes and colours he used in some of his abstract paintings. Look for pictures of interesting and unusual shaped buildings - describe where they can be seen and what they look like. Take a piece of A4 card and cut it into at least 5 different shapes. Try grouping the shapes together in different ways and draw round the group of shapes each time. Aim for at least three different arrangements. Finally stick the shapes into your sketchbook and describe each one. Draw a diagram of how to slot two shapes together. Make a quick sketch of your construction when you have made it.

Doing
Take a piece of A4 black card and a pair of scissors. You are going to cut it into several different shapes- more than four, but under ten! some of the shapes are needed to form a steady base on which the others will be added. Decide which pieces you are going to use and how they are going to fit together before you cut slits and slot them together. Now you can cut further slits and slot the other shapes on to the base to build a sculpture.
Look at your arrangement from different angles to see if it is interesting - you can always unslot the cut shapes and rearrange them until you are satisfied with the appearance of your construction. Choose a Kandinsky abstract painting, scissors and a piece of white card. Look at some of the shapes in the painting and either cut them out of the card freely without drawing or lightly sketch them on the card before cutting them out. Make the shapes fairly large as you need to paint them and slot them together. Mix the colours to match those of Kandinsky and decorate your shapes to match his - you will need to paint both sides of each shape as it will be viewed from different angles. When they are dry, slot the shapes together, remember to slot a firm base first before building upwards. Display the constructions with the pictures by Kandinsky.

Developing the Idea
• Make a class or group black card slotted construction.
• Make a class or group Kandinsky construction.
• Make a slotted card face.
• Make a slotted card animal or insect.
• Make a slotted construction based on a house.

Links with the work of Other Artists
Andy Goldsworthy
Sydney Opera House
Mondrian

Sculpture

Session   Six

Activity   Working with Wire

Focus   Line, Shape and Form

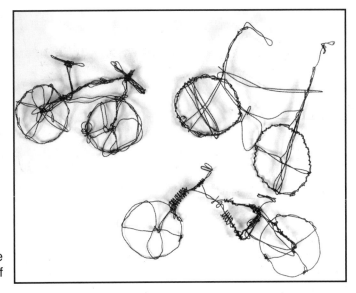

Equipment Needed

Flexiwire, drawing pencils (4b-6b), viewfinders, a bicycle (model or full size) to use as a stimulus, pictures of bicycles.

Talk About

- Making a loop at the end of each piece of wire before using it for safety sake.
- Bending the wire into different lines ie curves, zig-zags etc. including a loop or loops in a line.
- Making a complete circle and twisting the ends together to join them.
- Squashing a circle to make new shapes.
- Joining a line on to a circle by looping the end of it over the circle and twisting it together.
- Joining two circles together using several lines ie beginning to make a framework.
- This framework needs a lot of lines to make it firm.
- Doubling over the lines before they join on to give added strength.
- Adding and joining other shapes to the framework.
- The end result will be like a drawing (very linear) but in wire and in 3D.
- The different shapes on the bicycle, those that match the shapes you have already made with wire, and how those shapes are joined together.

Sketchbook Work

Make a collection of pictures of bicycles to stick on your page. Describe the wire you are going to use and how to use it safely. Draw some of the lines and shapes you can make with it. Describe how to join wire together - lines and circles. Use a drawing pencil to draw about four squares on your page, then with a view finder look at the different shapes on the bicycle and how they fit together. In each of your squares draw a different part of the bicycle. This will help you look more closely at the shapes you will need to make for your 3D drawing in wire. The pedals and the chain might be one drawing, the seat another, the handle bars another and finally one of the wheels.

Doing

Take several strands of flexiwire and loop the ends of each piece. Look at the actual bicycle again and decide which shape to make first. If you make the largest shape(s) first it will give you a guide as to size for the other shapes you need to join on. Lay the shapes on their side as you make them and work out how to join them together. The joins will need to be tight and firm or even double or the structure will fall apart. Some parts of your structure may need to made thicker than other parts and you will need to bend the wire over several times or use several strands of wire. Keep returning to look at the actual bicycle to make sure you make all the shapes - if you need detailed information your sketch book drawings should help you. When your structure is joined together, lift it up to see if it holds together firmly and intact. If not you will need to add in some extra pieces for strength. To display your completed 3D drawing of a bicycle upright you will need to make an extra support for it to prop it up on one side. Alternatively some of the wire bicycles could be hung on a white background whilst others stood up in front.

Developing the Idea

- Make a wire framework structure based on a model car - modern or vintage.
- Make a wire framework structure based on a model aircraft - modern or vintage.
- Make a wire framework structure based on a dinosaur.
- Make a wire framework structure based on a bird or insect.
- Make an abstract wire framework structure.

Links with the work of Other Artists

African Wire Structures
Willow frameworks in animal shapes to grow plants over
Andy Goldsworthy

Materials

Drawing pencils
wax crayons
Paint, paintbrushes
glue, glue spreaders
Masking tape, brown gummed tape
Card, reclaimed materials, fabric, yarn
Matchsticks, modroc, wire
FreeArt Paper 80 gsm
Scissors
Clay
Clay tools
Newspaper, tissue paper
Brusho or Easibrush dye

Suppliers

NES Arnold Ltd
Ludlow Hill Road
West Bridgeford
NOTTINGHAM
NG2 6HD

Pisces
Westwood Studies
West Avenue
CREWE
Cheshire
CW1 3AD

Philip & Tracey Ltd
North Way
Andover
Hampshire
SP10 5BA

Hope Education
Orb Mill
Huddersfield Road
OLDHAM
Lancashire
OL4 2ST

Yorkshire Purchasing Organisation
41 Industrial Park
WAKEFIELD
WF2 0XE

Sculpture

Session 1 Example of using another artist's 2D images as a starting point.

Session 2
Example of observational work on clay tiles.

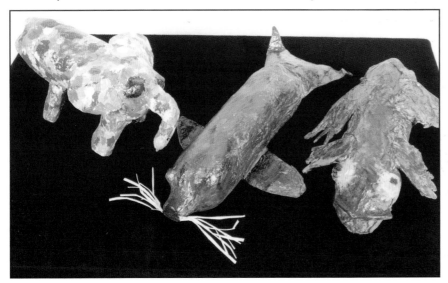

Session 3
Examples of adding and padding.

Sculpture

Session 4
An example of
further work with
newspaper.

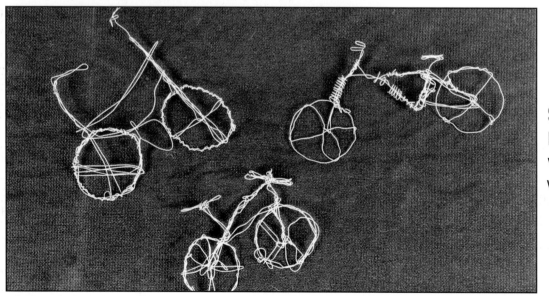

Session 5
An example of more
slotted structures.

Session 6
Examples of
working
with wire.

Textiles

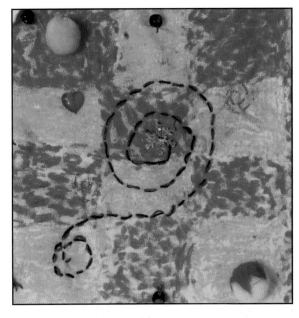

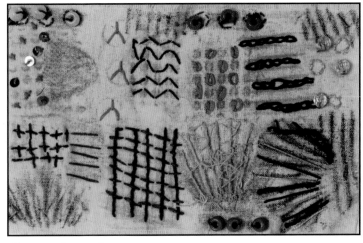

Session 1
Examples of rich rubbings.

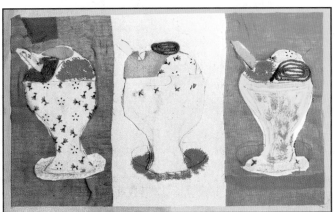

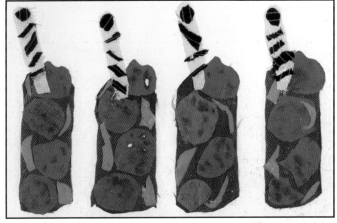

Session 2 Examples of choosing and combining.

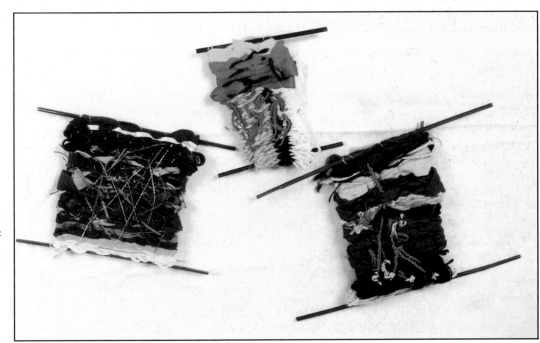

Session 3
Examples of
seasonal
weavings.

Textiles

Session 4
Examples of rag rug effects.

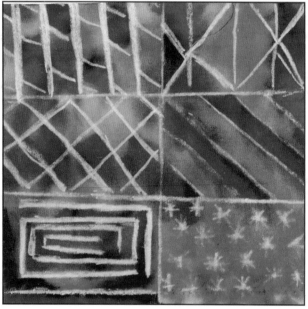

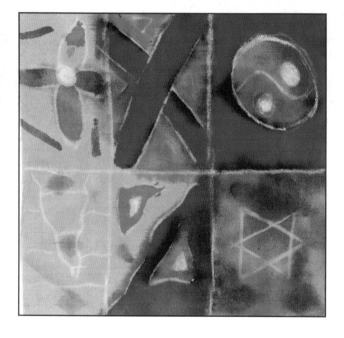

Session 5   Examples of wax resist.

Session 6
Example of soft sculptures.

Textiles

Textiles

Session   One

Activity   Rich Rubbings

Focus   Pattern, Colour and Texture.

Equipment Needed
White cotton fabric or plain pastel coloured fabric cut into pieces approx 20cm x 20 cm, Pental dye sticks or Markal oil based fabric markers or both, corrugated paper, embossed wall paper and other textured materials from which to take rubbings. Wax crayons and FreeArt paper 80gsm on which to test textured surfaces before working on fabric. Needles, threads, sequins and beads to develop the rubbings further. Card on which to make rubbing blocks for patterns and pictures for extension work.

Talk About
• Different textures eg smooth, bumpy, silky, bubbly etc
• Making a collection of objects and materials with different textures.
• Describing the different found textures and those from which rubbings could be taken.
• Taking rubbings with wax crayon on paper before working on fabric.
• Moving the textured surfaces around under the paper and fabric to encourage the rubbings to overlap and build up in richness.
• Experimenting with overlapping rubbings of different colours and textures.
• Adding to the rubbings with stitching, beads and sequins etc to emphasise the design.
• Arranging the stitches in groups or singly, and the beads in groups, rows of beads and as single beads on their own.
• Selecting colours and embellishments carefully - less is best! Beware of over kill!

Sketchbook Work
Make a list of some of the different textures that have been described and collected. Collect samples of fabrics and papers to stick on your page and describe the texture of each one. Collect magazine pictures that show different textures eg furry animals, rocks etc. Use wax crayon and FreeArt paper to take rubbings of some of the found textures. Cut them up to go in your sketchbook and record what you rubbed over to make each one. Try overlapping some of the rubbings to discover a richness of colour and pattern.

Doing
Look at the rubbings you have collected in your sketchbook and decide on those that have been the most successful and that you now want to repeat on fabric. Collect the textured materials from which each of these rubbings came. Get a piece of plain fabric and some dye sticks or Markal markers. Look at your piece of fabric before you start and decide where the rubbings are going to go, how many colours you are going to use and which colours they are going to be. Place your first piece of textured material under the fabric and begin your rubbing. Gradually build up the design with other or repositioned textures and the introduction of your other colours. When the fabric is rich in colour and pattern, cease rubbing and look at your design to decide where you are going to enhance and build it up further with groups or rows of stitches and groups and rows of sequins and/or beads. Position these on the design before stitching to make sure you are happy with the arrangement. The stitches might be in colours that blend in with the colours of the rubbings or contrast and clash with them - you decide!

Developing the Idea
• Arrange the textured material under the fabric to form an actual pattern.
• Stick the textured materials on a piece of card as a pattern so that it can be arranged and rubbed in a row or in a grid to make a repeat pattern.
• Stick textured material on a piece of card in the shape of an animal, a flower or a fish. Take a rubbing then embellish it further with stitches and beads.
• Stick textured material on a piece of card to form a picture eg a house, a landscape with trees etc. Rub in appropriate colours then embellish further as before.

Links with the work of Other Artists
Jan Beany
Ruth Issett
Belinda Downes.

Textiles

Session Two

Activity Choosing and Combining

Focus Colour, Shape, Pattern and Texture.

Equipment Needed

Pentel Dye sticks, Brusho or Easibrush powdered dye, Food colouring, yarns of different colours, thicknesses and textures. Plain coloured fabric, patterned fabric, felt, net, beads, needles and coloured threads, scissors, fabric glue, straight pins, pom-poms, white fabric in a choice of sizes for finished work eg 30cm x35cm or 20cm x25cm, Pictures of ice-cream sundaes in cones or glasses and pictures of highly decorated cakes on plates for stimulus. The book 'YUM YUM' which features Andy Warhol pictures of decorative food is an ideal stimulus/discussion starting point. Small pieces of white fabric on which to re-visit and try out previous textile techniques.

Talk About

• Textile techniques used before and how to do them eg dip and dye using food colouring, sprinkling dry powdered dye on to wet fabric, drawing on plain fabric, extending and enriching pattern by drawing on patterned fabric, overlaying net, sewing on beads, drawing with stitches, unravelling, plaiting and finger knitting yarn, folding and pleating fabric etc.
• The shapes and sizes of the ice-creams and their cones or glasses and the shapes and sizes of the cakes and their plates or cake stands.
• The colours and textures of the each group of foods and how these fit together.
• The additional decorations on each display of food eg flowers, cherries etc.
• Choosing, using and combining lots of different materials and techniques to create an image of a decorated cake or an ice-cream on a white fabric background. Arranging and pinning shapes in place before sewing or gluing them to decide on the most satisfying arrangement.

Sketchbook Work

Collect pictures of decorative cakes and ice creams from magazines to stick on your page. Find out and record details about the artist Andy Warhol. List the textile techniques that you have done and how to do them. Record how to do those that are new. Make several rough outline sketches of either cakes or ice creams from your pictures or from the Andy Warhol book. Draw some designs using these ideas in different combinations to create your own cakes or ice-creams. One of these you will develop further in a piece of finished textile work using a range of materials and techniques.

Doing

Choose a piece of white fabric to be the background and look at it carefully to decide how tall and how wide your fabric food is going to be, how much of the fabric it is going to fill, where it is going to be placed and where the container it sits on or in is going to go. Use the design you have chosen from your sketchbook to help. You now need to choose the fabrics you want to use, and begin cutting and arranging them, colouring and adding others to get the initial shapes of the food and the container it sits in or on. Pin them in place before you stitch or glue them. Look at the arrangement of shapes to decide where to add further decoration ie drawing, stitching or embellishing with beads etc. Are added textures or overlaying needed for added interest?

Write a description of your Fantastic Food when it is finished to describe its taste and ingredients! These could be included in the display.

Developing the Idea

• Design a cake or an ice-cream for a specific occasion eg Bonfire Night.
• Design a cake or an ice-cream for a story book character.
• Design a cake or an ice-cream for a person with a specific hobby or interest eg gardening, surfing etc.
• Design a cake or an ice cream for a specific artist.

Links with the work of Other Artists

Jan Beaney
Belinda Downes
Jean Littlejohn

Textiles

Session Three

Activity Seasonal Weavings

Focus Colour and Texture

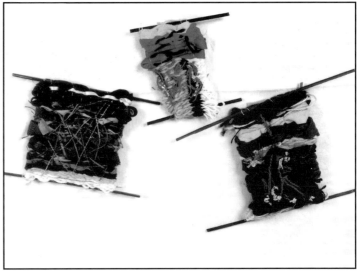

Equipment Needed
Strips of plain coloured fabric, coloured yarns, string, garden twine, raffia, pipe cleaners, buttons, beads, strips of lace, sequins, coloured ribbon, cut up coloured polythene bags, coloured crepe paper, sewing needles, fabric glue, coloured felt, cardboard looms for individual work, old bicycle wheels for group work. Magazines for seasonal pictures. Pieces of dowelling or strips of thick card to attach the warp threads to - top and bottom - when the initial weaving has been made and before adding decoration.

Talk About
- How to wind warp threads on to a cardboard loom to get it ready for weaving.
- How to weave the weft threads in and out of the warp to create a weaving.
- Weaving with fabric strips first to create the bulk of the weaving.
- Weaving - over these- with threads and yarns for added interest and texture.
- Taking the weaving off the loom and tying it on to doweling at either end before adding details.
- Sewing on buttons, beads or sequins in groups or individually to add interest.
- Making fringes, tassels, pompoms and plaits to add on to the design.
- Cutting appropriate shapes for the season eg icicles, sunbursts, raindrops etc out of coloured felt and stitching them on to the design.
- The names of the four seasons and colours appropriate to each one.
- Making a group weaving on a bicycle wheel and adding detail on to that.

Sketchbook Work
Draw a diagram and describe how to string up a loom. Name the different threads and how to weave. Make a list of things that are woven on a loom - add pictures from magazines if you can. Collect magazine pictures that are appropriate for each of the four seasons. Choose the one that you want to work from and stick it on your page. Next to your picture list the colours you can see in it plus any others you think match your chosen season. Make a list and some quick outline sketches of some of the shapes you might add and that are appropriate to your season. Some of these may be in your magazine picture.

Doing
Take a cardboard loom and string it up ready for weaving. Look at the fabric, lace, ribbons, crepe paper etc available to weave with and choose those that match your picture and your list in your sketchbook. Cut the fabric into strips so that it can be woven with. Choose your first colour and begin weaving on your loom - if you have fabric left over at the end of one row or several rows it can be turned to the back and stitched or stuck down once the weaving is complete and comes off the loom. Continue your weaving with your chosen strips of the various materials until the loom is full - remember to push the strips closely together and not to leave gaps. You may now want to weave over some of the fabric background with coloured yarns for added interest. When your weaving is complete, cut it carefully from the loom leaving enough of the warp threads at both the top and the bottom to tie each end to a piece of dowelling to keep it intact. Sew or stick any extra weft threads down - you now have a woven background to decorate in the theme of your season. Look at what you might sew on eg beads, how they might be arranged and also at what you might make from yarns eg fringes to add on plus shapes you might cut from felt to stick or sew on to complete your seasonal weaving.
Try working as a group in the same way on a bicycle wheel. This will make a circular weaving which will have to stay on its loom even when it is decorated!

Developing the Idea
- Use the colours and shapes from an abstract painting as the theme for a weaving.
- Make a weaving based on the colours and shapes suggested by a poem or a piece of music.
- Make a weaving based on a descriptive title eg the storm.
- Make a weaving based on a feeling eg anger, fear etc.

Links with the work of Other Artists
Michael Brennand Wood
Kaffe Fassett

Textiles

Session   Four

Activity   Rag Rug Effects

Focus   Colour, Shape, Pattern and Texture

Equipment Needed

Coloured fabric both patterned and plain, Polystyrene ceiling tiles or thick squares of polystyrene (NOT Press-Print or similar printing material) scissors, Marvin or PVA type glue, glue spreaders, matchsticks, drawing pencils (4b-6b). Wax crayons for sketchbook work.

Talk About

- Discuss making groups of three or four colours of fabric that link together in some way ie a group of warm colours, cold colours, a colour family.
- Sorting the patterned and plain fabric into the previously decided groups - patterned and plain fabric can go in the same group under one heading eg cold colours.
- Cutting the fabric into approx 4cm squares before starting work and making sure there are plenty of them!
- Drawing the outline of the design with a pencil on the polystyrene tile before adding the fabric.
- Putting a blob of glue on the back of each of the fabric squares with a glue spreader before using it.
- Gluing and working with one square at a time - not putting glue on all of them first.
- Putting the glued surface on to the tile and pushing it into the tile with a matchstick.
- Putting the squares closely together without leaving gaps.
- Following and filling the design drawn on the tile.

Sketchbook Work

Look at the groups that the fabrics have been sorted into. Draw a square on your page for each group and in it write the names of the colours and match them as closely as possible using wax crayons. Collect pictures of things that are circular and have patterns on them eg beach balls, marbles, beads etc. Choose the group of colours you want to work with and colour a block of each one using wax crayon - like a paint shade card. Now draw a series of circles on your page with a drawing pencil and add a different pattern to each one eg segments from the centre, stripes, concentric circles etc. Finally add your chosen group of colours to each pattern using wax crayons. You are going to choose one of these for your piece of work on the tile.

Doing

Take a polystyrene tile and on it roughly sketch the design you have chosen from your sketchbook, using a drawing pencil. It will need to be quite large - the outline of the circle shape itself should fill most of the tile. Once your design has been drawn you will need to collect the fabric you are going to use and begin cutting it into 4cm squares using scissors. As soon as you have a pile of squares you can put glue on the back of one, decide where it is going in your pattern and push it into the tile using a matchstick. Then glue up the next one and push that in place close to the first one and so on. Follow the pattern you have drawn with the different colours you have chosen, changing them when the design changes shape and using groups of patterned fabric for certain areas as well as plain for an interesting and varied arrangement.

Developing the Idea

- All the class work at creating their own individual circular patterns but using the same group of colours.
- Each child to create a stripey pattern that completely fills their tile - combine the tiles for a stripey textured large scale display!
- Create a circular design using the colours taken from a flower head.
- Create a design using grey, black and white only and no colour.
- Colour some of your own fabric to cut up and use.

Links with the work of Other Artists

Patchwork Quilts
Actual Rag Rugs
Kaffe Fassett

Textiles

Session   Five

Activity   Wax Resist

Focus   Colour, Pattern and Texture

Equipment Needed

White cotton fabric ready prepared for textile work (available from NES Arnold) cut in approx 20 cm squares, coloured cotton fabric cut in a similar way, white wax crayons (Berol Cascade are ideal) or any soft rich type of wax crayon, coloured wax crayons similarly soft and rich (Berol Cascade are again ideal), bottles of food colouring, paintbrushes, drawing pencils (4b-6b) masking tape, paper towels.

Talk About

- Taping the white fabric square on to the table top to keep it steady whilst it is being drawn on.
- Using white fabric and white wax crayons only to start with.
- Drawing firmly and applying plenty of wax.
- Adding lots of drawing to create interest on the surface of the fabric.
- Predicting what might happen when food colouring is painted on.
- Painting the different colours of food colouring on to the fabric with a brush and watching what emerges.
- A similar technique to this is Batik - here a batik pot is needed to heat the wax and the drawing is done with a tjanting tool (a small bowl with a spout, on a stick) . Batik differs in that several layers of drawing and colouring are built up on top of each other and the final layer is creased to give a crackled effect.

Sketchbook Work

Look up the word Batik and write down what it means and how it is done. Describe the approach you are going to use and how it is similar to Batik.

You are going to draw a pattern of different lines on your fabric - collect different sorts of lines by looking around the room, imagining lines, and looking at lines in the drawings made by book illustrators and other artists.

Next to each of the lines you draw try and think of a word to describe it and write it next to the line. Draw four or five squares on your page and in each one choose three or four of your lines to draw and become a pattern. You will be able to make your pattern more interesting if some of the lines are thicker than others, some are close together and some are further apart, some may even criss cross one another or go diagonally. You will need several different designs then you can choose the one you like best to become your pattern on the piece of fabric. Collect magazine pictures and pieces of actual fabric that have line patterns on them to add to your page.

Doing

Take a piece of white fabric and a white wax crayon. Tape your piece of fabric to the table with strips of masking tape on each edge. This will stop it moving around whilst you are drawing. Look at the line pattern you are going to use from your sketchbook and draw it carefully on to your piece of fabric. Press firmly as you draw as you need to transfer plenty of wax on to the fabric. Once your design is drawn, lift the fabric up and place a paper towel under it to stop the food colouring from staining the table. You are now ready to paint on the food colouring and reveal your line pattern. Paint the colours on carefully and arrange them so that they become a pattern too.

Now choose a piece of coloured fabric, draw the same, or if you want use another of your sketchbook designs and paint this with food colouring. Look for the differences that have occurred by using the same colours but on a coloured background. Display all the line designs together as though they were a large patchwork quilt.

Developing the Idea

- Divide your square of fabric into smaller squares and in each one draw a different sort of line. Colour each of the smaller squares with a different colour - you will need to repeat the colours but in different areas.
- Draw a picture instead of a pattern.
- All the class draw a shape eg a daisy head from observation and colour it in the same group of colours. They could be stitched or taped together to make a daisy wall hanging - add a yarn fringe along the bottom.
- Draw and colour an imaginary butterfly or fish for another themed class hanging - this time details could be added eg sequins, beads or stitching as extra decoration.

Links with the work of Other Artists

Examples of Fabric with Batik Patterns on them
Adire cloth from Africa

Textiles

Session   Six

Activity   Soft Sculpture

Focus   Colour and Shape

Equipment Needed

Old socks, tights, gloves, mittens, yarn, threads, needles, buttons, sequins, braid, pieces of felt, feathers, beads, pipe cleaners, wadding, cut up net curtains or pieces of foam to use as stuffing, fabric glue. Pictures of insects, birds, illustrations in story books featuring aliens and monsters to use as stimulus for an imaginary creature.

Talk About

- Using a ready made shape as a starting point.
- What these shapes are and how they are different and can be stuffed and used in different ways eg all the fingers of a glove or just a few.
- Filling the shape with stuffing.
- Not over filling the shape or it will be unable to be altered.
- Fastening the end of the shape so that the stuffing does not come out!
- Deciding what the shape could become and how it needs changing or altering.
- Altering parts of the shape by tying off or gathering and pulling stitches tightly round part of the shape.
- Adding details, decoration and character to the stuffed shape by sticking and stitching.
- The sort of features you might want to add eg noses, ears, legs, tails, feelers, wings, patterns etc.

Sketchbook Work

Collect pictures of unusual insects and birds from magazines - choose some to stick in your book. Look for storybook illustrations of aliens and monsters, sketch three or four of them into your book. Describe what you have drawn and where you found the pictures. You will need to draw more rough ideas later after you have stuffed your shape and are deciding how to change it into an imaginary creature. Make a list of all the materials you have to choose from and how the basic shape will be made.

Doing

Choose your found shape - a glove or a sock etc -and fill it with some stuffing (remember NOT TOO much!) and stitch up the end so that the stuffing doesn't fall out. Look carefully at your shape and think about how it might be altered and made more interesting by tying or stitching parts so that they separate from the whole. You could experiment with elastic bands before making the final ties or stitches. Once you have changed your stuffed shape draw it in your sketchbook - First how it was when it was first stuffed and secondly how it is now. Next you need to decide how to decorate and give character to this stuffed creature. Make a list of features you want to add to your stuffed shape and what you might make them out of. You may want to try eg several ideas /materials for noses before you have the one you want to use. You will also need to decide how you are going to attach these features (by sewing or sticking) and where they are going to go! Don't add too much or the identity of the final creature will be lost in a jungle of decoration! Draw a picture of your finished creature in your sketchbook and describe it. Write a story or description of each type of creature. Its habitat and habits could be included in the display.

Developing the Idea

- Make a camouflaged creature to sit in an open ended shoe box that is similarly camouflaged.
- Make an imaginary creature from the depths of the sea for a combined underwater display.
- Cut, stitch, assemble and stuff your own self made shapes from felt to make an abstract soft sculpture.
- Make a soft sculpture to match an item of food eg a hot dog or a licquorice allsort

Links with the work of Other Artists

Claus Oldenburg
Christo
Stuffed soft toys and inflatable toys
Max Ernst

Materials

White cotton Fabric
Pental Dye Sticks
Markal Markers
Wax crayons
FreeArt Paper 80 gsm
Needles
Threads
Sequins, beads, lace, crepe paper, ribbon, yarns
Brusho or Easibrush Dye
Food colouring
Felt, net
Pom-poms
Scissors
Fabric glue
Polystyrene ceiling tiles
PVA glue
Coloured fabric
Paintbrushes
Pipe cleaners, wadding

Suppliers

NES Arnold Ltd
Ludlow Hill Road
West Bridgeford
NOTTINGHAM
NG2 6HD

Pisces
Westwood Studies
West Avenue
CREWE
Cheshire
CW1 3AD

Philip & Tracey Ltd
North Way
Andover
Hampshire
SP10 5BA

Hope Education
Orb Mill
Huddersfield Road
OLDHAM
Lancashire
OL4 2ST

Yorkshire Purchasing Organisation
41 Industrial Park
WAKEFIELD
WF2 0XE